Chicken Soup for the Soul®
Christmas Treasury for Kids

CHICKEN SOUP FOR THE SOUL® CHRISTMAS TREASURY FOR KIDS

A Story a Day from December 1st Through Christmas for Kids and Their Families

Jack Canfield
Mark Victor Hansen
Patty Hansen
Irene Dunlap

Health Communications, Inc.
Deerfield Beach, Florida

www.hcibooks.com
www.chickensoup.com

We would like to acknowledge the following individuals who granted us permission to reprint the cited material.

The Easter Egg Christmas. Reprinted by permission of Denise Peebles. ©1999 Denise Peebles.

Lights for Lena. Reprinted by permission of Karen L. Garrison. ©2002 Karen L. Garrison.

My Christmas Wish. Reprinted by permission of Megan McKeown and Paul McKeown. ©2002 Megan McKeown.

An Unlikely Angel. Reprinted by permission of Crystal Ward Kent. ©2002 Crystal Ward Kent.

(Continued on page 115)

Library of Congress Cataloging-in-Publication Data

Chicken soup for the soul Christmas treasury for kids : a story a day
   from December 1st through Christmas for kids and their families /
   Jack Canfield . . . [et al.].
      p. cm.
   Summary: A collection of stories for each day in December through
Christmas Day, to rekindle the excitement of the season and remind us
what Christmas is really about.
      ISBN-13: 978-0-7573-0038-7 (hard cover)
      ISBN-10: 0-7573-0038-3 (hard cover)
      ISBN-13: 978-0-7573-0690-7 (trade paper)
      ISBN-10: 0-7573-0690-X (trade paper)
      1. Christmas—Juvenile literature. [1. Christmas.] I. Canfield, Jack, date.

GT4985.5 .C45 2002
394.2663—dc21

                                                                2002069077

HCI, its logos and marks are trademarks of Health Communications, Inc.

Publisher: Health Communications, Inc.
            3201 S.W. 15th Street
            Deerfield Beach, FL 33442-8190

Cover design by Larissa Hise Henoch
Inside formatting by Dawn Von Strolley Grove

This book is dedicated to
Gabby and Dee Dee Romanello . . .
your example of reading Christmas stories together
inspired this book.
We also dedicate this book to our children . . .
we love reading with you,
and hope that someday you will pass
this family tradition
on to your own children.
Blessings and love.

DENNIS THE MENACE

"WHAT CAN AN **ALMOST** GOOD BOY GET FOR CHRISTMAS?"

Contents

Acknowledgments

During our production of *Chicken Soup for the Soul Christmas Treasury for Kids*, we were blessed with the helping hands and generous hearts of many people, who made it a delight to bring it into being. We want to acknowledge all of you who aided in the creation of this book, as well as those people in our lives who sustain our souls and bodies during book production.

Our families, who always support us in making the world a better place for all kids! Inga, Christopher, Oran and Kyle Canfield, Travis and Riley Mahoney, for all their love and backing of Jack's mission; Elisabeth and Melanie Hansen, for being the inspiration that fuels Mark and Patty's lives, and Shirley Shaw for her constant love; Eva Espinosa for keeping Billy quiet and her generous heart; Kent, Marleigh and Weston Dunlap for believing in our projects and being there for Irene, and Angela Jack for her unending love and encouragement.

Gina Romanello—what would we ever do without you? You are the answer to all of our prayers. With you picking up the ball and running with it, we can conquer any deadline! You know what to do to make whatever needs to happen come together. Thanks for constantly thinking on your feet, being flexible and working until the job is done, no matter what. You ROCK! Brittany Shaw, for always being there when we need you the most; Dee Dee Romanello, for going the extra mile and never complaining; Dawn Henshall, for your dedication to making sure that Patty stayed on track during book production. Taylor Nordgren, for helping out with whatever we needed done to get the book out on time.

Patty Aubery, for her great attitude while making sure the business of *Chicken Soup for the Soul* Enterprises, Inc., is handled with finesse. Russ Kamalski, for his enthusiastic collaboration; Ken Browning, without whom we would really be in trouble.

Our publisher, Peter Vegso, for his vision and commitment to *Chicken Soup for the Soul*.

Christine Belleris, editorial director, and Allison Janse, Lisa Drucker and Susan Tobias, our editors at Health Communications, Inc., and their assistant, Kathy Grant, for their devotion to excellence.

Terry Burke, Randee Feldman, Tom Sand, Irena Xanthos, Lori Golden, Kelly Johnson Maragni, Karen Bailiff Ornstein, Patricia McConnell, Kim Weiss, Maria Dinoia, Paola Fernandez-Rana and Teri Peluso, the marketing, sales, administration and PR departments at Health Communications, Inc., for doing such an incredible job supporting our books—a big thank-you!

Larissa Hise Henoch, director of the art department at Health Communications, Inc., who put together the wonderful cover for this book, and Lawna Patterson Oldfield, Andrea Perrine Brower, Lisa Camp, Anthony Clausi and Dawn Grove, the awesome creative team in the art department—you are fantastic!

Heather McNamara and D'ette Corona, for being there every step of the way during the production of our final manuscript. We love you both.

Leslie Riskin, for handling the numerous permissions

needed with grace and style. You deserve a medal!

Maria Nickless, for her zealous marketing and public-relations expertise.

Nancy Mitchell-Autio and Barbara LoMonaco, for their loving support with sending us stories and cartoons.

Laurie Hartman, for her enthusiastic marketing and management of the *Chicken Soup* brand and licenses.

Veronica Romero, Robin Yerian, Teresa Esparza, Vince Wong, Kristen Allred, Stephanie Thatcher, Kathy Brennan-Thompson, Dana Drobny, Michelle Adams, Lisa Williams, Trudy Marschall, Dave Coleman, Jody Emme, Carly Baird and Shanna Vieyra, for your commitment, dedication and professionalism in making sure Jack's, and Mark and Patty's offices run smoothly.

All the *Chicken Soup for the Soul* coauthors, who make it such a joy to be part of this *Chicken Soup* family: Raymond Aaron, Matthew E. Adams, Patty and Jeff Aubery, Nancy Mitchell-Autio, Marty Becker, John Boal, Cynthia Brian, Cindy Buck, Ron Camacho, Barbara Russell Chesser, Dan Clark, Tim Clauss, Barbara De Angelis, Don Dible, Mark and Chrissy Donnelly, Rabbi Dov Elkins, Bud Gardner, Jennifer Read Hawthorne, Kimberly Kirberger, Carol Kline, Tom and Laura Lagana, Tommy LaSorda, Janet Matthews, Hanoch and Meladee McCarty, Heather McNamara, Katy McNamara, Paul J. Meyer, Arline Oberst, Marion Owen, Maida Rogerson, Martin Rutte, Amy Seeger, Marci Shimoff, Sid Slagter, Barry Spilchuk, Pat Stone, Carol Sturgulewski, LeAnn Thieman, Jim Tunney, Diana von Welanetz Wentworth and Steve Zickman.

Our glorious panel of readers who helped us with the final selections. They read and evaluated each story with honesty and a commitment to help make this Christmas treasury the best book possible for their peers. Thanks to the following teachers and their classes: Joanne Harabedian, Pennie Grayson, Gayle Paige, Diane Hrstich,

Paulette Dobbs, Pinky Winston, Jennifer Brandewie, Jennifer Rogers, Colleen Peschell, Pam Huston, Carol Webb, Kathy Martell, Kathy Nelson, Nancy Dufour, Sue Griffith, Arbee Chambers, Bob Mueller, Joannie Sinnette, Dorothy Olender, Julie Cambonga and Jennifer Harabedian.

Lieutenant Colonel Tom Jones and Major George Hood, for your vision and for collaborating with us to bring more awareness to the Salvation Army Angel Tree Project.

And, most of all, we wish to acknowledge all of the kids, teachers, writers and others who submitted their heartfelt stories, poems and quotes for possible inclusion in this book. While we were not able to use everything you sent in, we know that each one came from a very special Christmas memory in your life.

We may have left out the names of some people who contributed along the way. If so, we are sorry, but please know that we really do appreciate you very much.

We are truly thankful and love you all!

Introduction

Ahhh . . . Christmas! The fresh smell of pine, cookies baking and a roasted turkey filled with stuffing. Tree decorations sparkle and shimmer in the lights. Last-minute shopping, Santa Claus in the mall and going Christmas caroling. Candlelight church service on Christmas Eve. Trying to stay awake long enough to hear reindeer on the roof. The big present that you've been wanting all year, other presents under the tree that tempt you to pick them up and shake them. Christmas stockings filled with candy, toys and books and underwear from your grandma (again!). It's all part of the holiday season.

But the most important of all is the magic that happens when love is shared this special time of the year . . . love for your fellow humans, your teachers and friends, and especially your family.

One of the best ways for a family to show love for one another is to spend time together. We encourage you to give a special gift to your family this season by reading these stories together—stories that show the true meaning of Christmas, each in its own way.

You are holding the only book that we know of where kids themselves have selected stories about Christmas that were written by other kids (and some adults who haven't forgotten what this special time of year means to kids!). To make sure that you will love the stories in this book, each one was carefully chosen by a readers panel of 350 kids, just like you, from all across the country. The one thousand or so stories that we received were narrowed down to the top twenty-five stories about the sharing of love, Christmas traditions, giving from the heart, holiday magic in the form of miracles and the meaning of the real spirit of Christmas.

Chicken Soup for the Soul Christmas Treasury for Kids will help you celebrate each day of the Christmas season one story a day starting December first through Christmas day.

Our highest hope is that you'll love each story as much as the kids who chose them did. We wish also that the magic and love that is found in the true meaning of Christmas is yours now . . . and evermore.

Merry Christmas!

Share with Us

We would love to hear your reactions to the stories in this book. Please let us know what your favorite stories were and how they affected you.

We are currently accepting submissions for *Chicken Soup for the Preteen Soul II* and *Chicken Soup for the Family Soul*. We invite you to send stories, poems and quotes that you would like to see published to:

Irene Dunlap and Patty Hansen
c/o LifeWriters
P.O. Box 10879
Costa Mesa, CA 92627
phone: 949-645-5240
fax: 949-645-3203
Web site: *www.LifeWriters.com*

You can also access other information and find a current list of other planned *Chicken Soup* books at the *Chicken Soup for the Soul* Web site, *www.chickensoup.com.* Check out *www.clubchickensoup.com* for information about our *Chicken Soup* online service. Go to *www.preteenplanet.com,* a difference-making Web site for kids aged nine to thirteen, for empowerment and fun.

What is Christmas?
It is tenderness for the past,
courage for the present,
hope for the future.
It is a fervent wish that every cup
may overflow with blessings
rich and eternal,
And that every path may lead to peace.

Agnes M. Pharo

The Easter Egg Christmas

Christmas is not a time nor a season, but a state of mind. To cherish peace and goodwill, to be plenteous in mercy, is to have the real spirit of Christmas.

Calvin Coolidge

Easter was just a week away when the radio announcements began. Each day, as the holiday approached, my five-year-old daughter, Ashley, and I would hear updates about the Easter egg hunts coming up at local parks in our area.

With the first mention of the events, Ashley began pleading with me to take her to one of the big egg hunts the coming weekend. I knew in my heart that sometimes events like these could set kids up for disappointment. With so many kids scrambling for only so many eggs, the odds of her not finding any at all were very real. Still, I did not want to be the reason why she might feel let down, so I smiled at her and agreed to take her, all the while hoping that she would be able to find at least one egg.

Saturday came and we drove to the hunt that Ashley had decided would be best. The parking lot was jammed with cars loaded with children. Frustrated by all the chaos, I considered leaving and just going home again when Ashley jumped out of the car with basket in hand, eager to begin hunting. She was not discouraged in the least by the crowds.

After I parked the car, I joined Ashley and as we began walking toward the event area we heard an announcement on the loud speaker. The Easter Bunny had hidden hundreds of eggs early that morning, and each and every one contained a surprise inside. Ashley's eyes lit up as she imagined what treasure she might find inside the special eggs.

I glanced across the field that was roped off for the hunt and was easily able to see several eggs lying out in the open area. To make sure that the hunt was fair for kids of all ages, the field was roped off in sections and each section had an age limit. Ashley signed in and was directed to the proper line for her age group. When the whistle blew and the rope was dropped, the children ran into the field searching quickly for all the eggs they could find. After the hunt was officially over, each child began his journey back across the field.

Disappointment showed on the faces of the children who didn't find any eggs. Huge smiles were on those who did. I searched the crowd for Ashley, growing concerned that she might be in the group of children who didn't find anything. I hoped that her heart had not been broken.

Just then, I spotted her in the distance running toward me with her basket. To my relief, she was smiling. Once she reached me, I counted three eggs lying in her basket. She plopped down on the grass and reached for one, which she quickly twisted open.

The egg contained a certificate for a Happy Meal™

compliments of McDonald's. That made her day right there, regardless of what else might be in the other two eggs. We decided we'd go there for lunch.

The second egg rattled when she shook it. The mystery was quickly solved when several golden tokens to Chuck E. Cheese Pizza Palace fell from the plastic egg. Ashley looked up at me with pleading eyes and asked if we could go there and play for a while after we ate at McDonald's. I agreed as she reached for the last egg.

I didn't think that anything would top what she had found in the first two eggs until we saw it with our own eyes. There, inside egg number three, was a gift certificate to Toys "R" Us for fifty dollars!

Ashley had won the grand prize!

She jumped up and down, thrilled, as I expected she would be. But I had no idea that her happiness wasn't simply because she had won a toy-shopping spree until we got in the car.

"Mommy, can we stop by the mall on the way home?" Ashley asked.

I assumed that she wanted to spend her gift certificate, and I agreed. As I buckled her into her seat, I quizzed her on what toy she had in mind.

"I don't want any toys for me, Mom. I want to buy some toys for an angel," she replied.

"An angel?" I questioned. I couldn't understand what she was talking about. And then I remembered what had happened during the previous holiday season.

Last Christmas, Ashley and I had been doing our Christmas shopping in the mall. We came upon a gigantic tree in the middle of the mall with paper angels hanging from the tree branches. Each angel had the name of a child written on it. Ashley asked me what they were for. I explained that sometimes Santa can't visit every child's

house on Christmas Eve, so he sends a list of kids to the
Salvation Army. They put the names on angels and hang
them on this special tree in the mall. That way, people can
help Santa out by giving presents to one of the children
whose name is on an angel. The tree is called an Angel Tree.

Ashley just stood there, looking at the tree and all
the names hanging there. Distracted with thoughts of
completing my Christmas shopping and thinking that I
had satisfied her curiosity, I rushed her off so I could finish
looking for the items I had on my Christmas list.

Later that night, as Ashley was getting ready for bed,
she wanted to know what happens to the angels who no
one buys presents for. "Will they get any toys?" she asked.

I explained that the Salvation Army would try and see
to it that every child would have a visit from Santa on
Christmas. Her concern touched me so much that I suggested we say a special prayer for every kid whose name
was on the Angel Tree. So we offered a prayer that all of
the Angel Tree children would get presents for Christmas.
She closed her eyes and drifted off to sleep.

I had thought that was the end of it, but now, months
later, I realized that she had never forgotten about the
Angel Tree children. I pulled over to the side of the road
and looked into the eyes of this little girl sitting beside me.
Though small in size, her compassion for others was huge.
I explained to her that the Angel Tree is only in the mall at
Christmas and it was now Easter. There would be no
Angels to adopt at this time of year.

Ashley sat there in silence for a minute and then she
looked at me.

"Mommy, can we save this money until Christmas?"
she asked.

"Yes, we can," I answered. "And we will make some girl
or boy very happy!"

I looked at the excitement on Ashley's face and realized

that all along I had acted like Christmas was all about buying the right gifts for my family and friends, decorating our home and creating a wonderful Christmas dinner. It had taken my five-year-old daughter to make me realize that it is up to all of us to help the less fortunate, especially at Christmas. Her compassion woke me up to what the true spirit of Christmas is all about. As I pulled back onto the highway, I knew in my heart that I had developed a respect for my daughter that I would carry with me forever.

That next Christmas, Ashley and I went to the mall on the very first day that the Salvation Army put up the big, beautiful Angel Tree. We quickly picked out *two* Angels, one for Ashley and one for me, and with smiles on our faces we set off for an extra-special shopping trip.

That early December day, we began a Christmas tradition that all started because of an extraordinary Easter egg hunt and a little girl with a very big heart.

Denise Peebles

[EDITORS' NOTE: *Ashley is now seventeen years old and has been actively involved in the Salvation Army Angel Tree Project each year, wrapping and distributing gifts to children. In many cases, the Angel gifts are the only Christmas presents these children receive. To become involved in the Angel Tree Project in your area, call your local branch of the Salvation Army or go to* www.salvationarmyusa.org.]

DENNIS THE MENACE

"MY MOM SAID, 'THE BEST GIFT YOU CAN GIVE IS *YOURSELF!*'"

Lights for Lena

You give little when you give of your possessions. It is when you give of yourself that you truly give.

Kahlil Gibran

It had been the perfect winter night to view Christmas lights. "Hurry, kids!" I shouted upstairs to my children. "Daddy's already outside warming the van." Within minutes I heard excited voices. "Mommy! Mommy!" my six-year-old daughter Abigail shouted, sliding on her behind down the carpeted stairs. "Is the hot chocolate ready?"

"It's in the van," I told her, smiling as my two-year-old son Simeon tugged at my shirt. We were all wearing our pajamas. After all, this was a Christmas tradition! Each year at Christmastime, we'd get into our sleepwear, pack a bag full of munchies and head to our van to go looking at decorations on neighboring houses. We had just stepped out of the door when Abigail surprised me by asking, "Mama, can you give me more money for doing my chores? I want to buy you, Daddy and Simeon the best gifts for Christmas!"

"The best gifts are those that come from the heart," I grinned, recalling how she had drawn me a picture of a rainbow the previous day after learning I hadn't been feeling well.

"You mean that instead of buying people things at the stores, that there's other ways to give them gifts?"

"Yep," I answered, securing her seat belt. "All people have to do is look into their hearts, and they'll find many good gifts to give."

Settled into the van, we opened the bag of goodies, and the kids cheered as we passed house after house decorated with snowmen, Santa and his reindeer and nativity scenes, glowing brightly in Christmas lights.

Suddenly, it began snowing lightly just as we rounded the corner of a street that led into the neighborhood that my husband Jeff and I had lived in years before. The headlights flashed onto the first brick home of the street. The house appeared disturbingly dark compared to the bright lights displayed by its neighbors.

"The people who live there must not like Christmas," Abigail noted from the back seat.

"Actually, honey," my husband said, stopping the van briefly along the curb, "they used to have the best decorated house in the neighborhood." Jeff clasped my hand, and I sighed, remembering Lena and her husband and how they used to take such joy in decorating their home for Christmas. "It's for the children," they'd say. "We like to imagine them in the back seat of their parents' cars, their little faces full of Christmas magic as they look at our home."

"Why don't they decorate it anymore?" Abigail asked, bringing my attention to the present.

"Well," I began, remembering the dark days when Lena's husband had been hospitalized, "her husband died a few years ago, and Lena's very old. She only has one child, and he's a soldier living far away."

"Tell me what she's like," Abigail said, and for the next few minutes Jeff and I filled her in on the kind things Lena used to do.

"And every Sunday after church, she'd make home-made cookies and invite us over. She's an incredible person," Jeff concluded.

"Can we visit her now?" asked Abigail.

Simeon met Abigail's question with enthusiastic agreement, and I shared our children's excitement. Both Jeff and I looked down at our attire.

"I knew this would happen one day," he said, rubbing his forehead. "First I let you talk me into wearing pajamas in the van, and now you're going to want me to actually go visiting, right?"

I kissed his cheek and an hour later, after leaving Lena's home, Abigail and Simeon clutched the crocheted tree ornaments she'd graciously given them.

"I wish I had a gift for her," Abigail said, waving at the elderly woman standing in her doorway.

The next morning, my children gave me strict orders not to come upstairs. They said something about it being a secret mission for Christmas. After rummaging through drawers, closets and toy chests, they came down the stairs wearing toy construction hats, snow boots and Simeon's play tool belts.

"What is all this?" I laughed. "Are you going to fix things around here?"

"Nope," Abigail smiled brightly. "We're going to give a gift to Lena. Since she's too old and doesn't have anyone to do it for her, we're going to decorate her house for Christmas!"

Her words brought tears to my eyes. "That's a wonderful idea," I said, calling their father. "But I think you'll need Daddy and me to help. Is it okay if we're part of your secret mission?"

"Sure!" they replied. Hours later, we stood with Lena, who couldn't have been happier, on the sidewalk in front of her now brightly glowing house. The lights we had found in her basement were shining with pride over snow-capped arches and windows. Candy canes lined the sidewalk and welcomed passersby to the nativity scene that Abigail and Simeon had positioned on the snow-covered lawn. A car cruising along slowed its speed to view the lights. Two children peeked from the back window, their faces full of excitement. Lena watched them, her eyes aglow.

It had been a day full of hard work, but it was worth every second to see the joy on Lena's face. Suddenly, she disappeared inside her home and returned carrying a tray of freshly baked cookies.

Abigail reached her hand inside my coat pocket and clutched my fingers.

"You were right, Mom," she sighed, her dark eyes content.

"About what, sweetie?"

She leaned her head against my arm and replied, "The best gifts are those from the heart." I kissed the top of her head, so proud of her for using her own heart to think of this, and then I turned to my husband. Our eyes met and he smiled.

"Looks like decorating Lena's house can be added to our list of Christmas traditions," he announced. The kids heartily agreed.

Karen L. Garrison

My Christmas Wish

*H*ope deferred makes the heart sick, but when dreams come true, there is life and joy.

Proverbs 13:11–13

It became a very sad Christmas for us when we found out why Grandpa had been so sick lately. The doctors called my family to tell us that Grandpa had cancer. If that wasn't bad enough news, we learned that we wouldn't be able to have Christmas at home with him because he would be in the hospital getting treatment. We went to visit him on Christmas day, but he was too weak to really enjoy celebrating with us.

Over the next nine months, he was admitted to many hospitals and was continually moved from room to room: from ICU to private room, etc. I could hardly keep up with where he was.

One day, while Grandpa was watching TV in the hospital, he saw a commercial with a Jack Russell terrier that was shown flying through the air to the slogan, "Life's a journey—enjoy the ride." Grandpa fell in love. When my Uncle Shane went to visit him, Grandpa wouldn't stop talking about "that cute little dog on the commercial." To humor him, Uncle Shane found a picture of a Jack Russell terrier just like the one in the commercial. He brought it to the hospital and hung it on the wall of my grandfather's room. Whenever Grandpa moved to another room, he brought the picture with him.

By September, Grandpa wasn't improving like the doctors expected he would, so they told him he should see a special doctor in Dallas. Everyone agreed, and Grandpa was flown by air ambulance to another hospital in Texas.

One day, as we were chatting with him on the phone, Grandpa told us, "I want a Jack Russell terrier, and I am going to get one when I get well." We realized then that the thought of getting a little terrier was encouraging him to keep going and was giving him hope.

Months passed and Grandpa had several surgeries to help him beat the cancer. He was still very weak, so I wondered if he would be home for Christmas. As December arrived, having Grandpa home with us on Christmas became the only thing I wished for. Every night, I prayed that my wish would come true.

Then right before Christmas, the doctors said he could go home. With some help from Uncle Shane, my grandpa would be able to leave the hospital and begin his journey back home.

My whole family was excited to get the news. It had been a long, hard year for all of us. Since Grandpa would be coming home on Christmas Eve, everyone wanted to do something extra special for him this year. As soon as a Jack Russell terrier was mentioned, we knew that it was the surprise that would really make Grandpa happy. It was the kind of dog that Grandpa had looked at every day on his hospital wall, the dog that kept my grandpa hoping to get well. So, for days, my mom, uncles and aunts searched the ads in the papers looking for a real Jack

Russell terrier puppy to give to Grandpa.

Finally, the day before Christmas Eve, we found a home that had Jack Russell terrier puppies for sale. I helped pick out just the right one that I knew would make my grandpa very happy.

The following evening, as we were sitting by the fire playing with the puppy, we got a phone call from Uncle Shane saying that he and Grandpa were stuck in New York City because of a storm. They wouldn't be making it home that night. We were all so disappointed. Before I fell asleep, I prayed once again that Grandpa would make it home for Christmas. He was so close!

I woke up Christmas morning to wonderful presents under the tree. But even though they were all things that I liked, they didn't make up for not having Grandpa home. Throughout the day, my family waited anxiously to hear from Uncle Shane again. Finally, we couldn't take it any-more and decided to just go over to Grandpa's house and wait there. We played games, did jigsaw puzzles and tried to enjoy the day, but by late in the afternoon, we were get-ting sadder by the minute.

Then suddenly, we heard someone coming up the front stairs. I peeked out the front door to see my uncle holding my grandpa in his arms. He had to carry him because he was so weak from the long trip.

We all screamed when they came through the door. They were finally home! Suddenly, the puppy began bark-ing from all of the excitement. You should have seen the look on my grandpa's face. I can't remember seeing him smile that big in my life. He was so happy! All night long, the puppy, which he named Tara, and Grandpa, snuggled together in Grandpa's favorite chair.

Before Christmas day had ended, the only thing I had wished for had come true.

Grandpa was home.

Megan McKeown, twelve

An Unlikely Angel

Kindness is the golden chain by which society is bound together.

Johann von Goethe

It was just before Christmas. An angry middle-aged man stood at the counter of the animal shelter, gripping the leash of an aging German shepherd. "Why won't you take him?" he shouted. "I need to get him off my hands!"

The adoption counselor tried once more to explain. "At fourteen, Samson is too old to be a good adoption candidate," she said.

"Well, then just take him and put him down," the man yelled. "I want to be rid of him."

"We don't take animals just to put them down," the counselor explained. "May I ask why you no longer wish to keep the dog?"

"I just can't stand the sight of him," the man hissed, "and if you won't put him down, I'll shoot him myself."

Trying not to show her horror, the counselor pointed out that shooting an animal was illegal. She urged the man to consult with his veterinarian for other options.

"I'm not spending any more money on this animal," the man grumbled and, yanking the leash, he stalked out.

Concerned, the counselor wrote down the license plate of the man's truck and offered up a quick prayer for Samson.

A few days later, a German shepherd was found abandoned. He was brought to the shelter, and the staff recognized him as Samson. The town where he had been abandoned was where his owner lived. The man was contacted by the police and, under questioning, admitted that distraught over his recent divorce, he had sought revenge through the shepherd. He hadn't even wanted the dog, but he fought to keep him to spite his wife. Once his wife was gone, he couldn't bear to see the animal. The man was charged with abandonment, and Samson came to stay at the shelter.

The wife and the couple's son were located in Pennsylvania. They were horrified to hear what had happened to their dog and agreed immediately to have him come live with them.

There was just one problem: The wife was nearly broke after the divorce and their initial move. She could take no time off from work to drive to New Hampshire and get the dog, and she couldn't afford any other method of getting him to her. She hated to have Samson in the shelter any longer but didn't know what to do. "We'll come up with something," the staff assured her, but in their hearts they didn't know what. They were concerned, as well. Samson had lived with his family all his life. Within a few weeks, his whole world had been turned upside down. He was beginning to mope, and the staff could tell by his eyes that if he wasn't back with his family soon, he would give up.

Christmas was only two weeks away when the angel arrived. He came by pickup truck in the form of a man in his mid-thirties. Through a friend of a shelter staffer, he had heard about Samson's plight. He was willing to drive Samson to Pennsylvania, and he would do it before Christmas.

The staff was thrilled with the offer, but cautious. Why would a stranger drive hundreds of miles out of his way to deliver a dog to people he didn't know? They had to make sure he was legitimate and that Samson wouldn't be sold to meat dealers or dumped along the interstate.

The man understood their concerns and, thankfully, checked out to be an upstanding citizen. In the course of the conversation, he explained why he had come forward.

"Last year, I left my dog in my van while I went to do some grocery shopping," he explained. "While I was inside, the van caught fire. I heard people hollering and rushed out to see my van engulfed in flames. My dog meant everything to me, and he was trapped. I tried to get to the van, but people restrained me. Then I heard someone shouting, 'The dog is safe! The dog is safe!' I looked over, and there was this man I'd never seen before, holding my dog. He had risked his own life to get my dog out. I'll forever be in his debt. Just when you don't think there are heroes any more, one comes along.

"I vowed then and there that if I ever had the chance to do someone a good turn when it came to a beloved pet, that I would. When I heard about Samson and his family, I knew this was my chance, so here I am."

The shelter staff was amazed. They all knew about the van rescue story. It had been in all the papers, and the shelter had even given the rescuer a reward, but they had never dreamed that Samson's angel was connected to this earlier good deed.

A few days later, Samson and his angel were on their way. The dog seemed to know he was going home, because his ears perked up and his eyes were brighter than they had been in some time.

Just before Christmas, the mail brought one of the best cards the shelter had ever received. Along with a thank-you note were photos of a deliriously happy Samson romping with his family in the snow and snuggling with them by their Christmas tree. Samson was truly where he belonged, and the staff knew he would live out his days happily there.

They also knew that Samson's journey home was a true Christmas miracle, and that angels—and heroes—may still appear when you need them, even in the most unlikely forms.

Crystal Ward Kent

I'm Not Scrooge . . . I'm Just Broke!

Creativity is inventing, experimenting, growing, taking risks, breaking rules, making mistakes and having fun.

Mary Lou Cook

It's said that you can never have too many friends, but Christmas was just a week away and I had five people left to shop for on my Christmas list and only three dollars to my name. How do you tell your mother, brother and three friends that you can only spend sixty cents on each of them?

"Let's set a price limit on our gifts this year," I suggested to my best friend, Joanie.

"That's a good idea," Joanie agreed. "How about nothing over five dollars?"

"How about nothing over sixty cents?" I felt like the biggest cheapskate in the world.

"I guess this is where I'm supposed to say it's not the gift, it's the thought that counts," Joanie smiled. "But don't blame me if all you get is a stick of gum!"

It is almost impossible to buy anything for under sixty

cents, so it was really going to have to be very small gifts with very big thoughts. I'd never spent so much time or effort trying to come up with the right gift for the right person.

Finally, Christmas day arrived, and I was worried how people would feel about my "cheap" gifts.

I gave my mother a scented candle with a note that said, "You are the brightest light in my life." She almost cried when she read the note.

I gave my brother a wooden ruler. On the back of it I'd painted, "No brother in the world could measure up to you." He gave me a bag of sugar and had written on it, "You're sweet." He'd never said anything like that to me before.

For Joanie, I painted an old pair of shoes gold and stuck dried flowers in them with a note that said, "No one could ever fill your shoes." She gave me a feather and a Band-Aid. She said I always tickled her funny bone and made her laugh until her sides ached.

To my other two friends, I gave one a paper fan and wrote on it, "I'm your biggest fan." To the other, I gave a calculator that cost one dollar and I painted a message on the back, "You can always count on me." They gave me a rusty horseshoe for luck and a bundle of sticks tied with a red ribbon because "friends stick together."

I don't remember all the other gifts that I got from people last Christmas, but I remember every one of the "cheap" gifts.

My brother thinks I'm sweet. My mother knows she is the most important person in my life. Joanie thinks I'm funny and I make her laugh, which is important because her dad moved away last year and she misses him and is sad sometimes.

I was worried I wouldn't have enough money for Christmas gifts, but I gave gifts to five people and still had twenty cents left over. We all still talk about our "cheap" gifts and how much fun it was to come up with a gift that cost pennies but told someone how we really felt about them. On my bookshelf, I still have a bag of sugar, a feather, a horseshoe and a bundle of sticks . . . and they are priceless.

Storm Stafford

DENNIS THE MENACE

"ALL MR. WILSON GOT FOR CHRISTMAS WAS A BUNCH OF CLOTHES. HE MUST HAVE BEEN *REALLY* NAUGHTY."

Helping Lauren

The joy of brightening other lives, bearing each other's burdens, easing other's loads and supplanting empty hearts and lives with generous gifts becomes for us the magic of Christmas.

W. C. Jones

It would be safe to say that I was definitely not looking forward to my first Christmas after moving to southern Georgia, away from the comforts of my home, friends and family back in Baltimore. Of course, I was looking forward to the presents, but in spite of the joys of the season, I approached Christmas skeptically. I missed the cold weather, the steaming mugs of hot cocoa, my best friends' annual Christmas party, our front hall with its gleaming tree and, most of all, Christmas at Grandma's house.

Our family would tramp into her warm kitchen, all six of us, after a long two-hour drive. The delicious aroma of cookies baking and the turkey roasting in the oven always made my mouth water. Grandma would bustle in with her apron covered in flour, smile and give us each a hug. She would cluck about how cold it was getting, pat us on the head and send us kids off to play. My three sisters and I would wait eagerly for our cousins to arrive. When they finally came, we would all rush down to the basement to discuss Christmas presents in secret.

Every Christmas, for as long as I can remember, that's what we did. But now that my family had moved, that Christmas tradition was gone. It was depressing, really; Christmas this year would be different. Yet I learned, with the help of a five-year-old girl named Lauren, that I'm not so unlucky after all.

School was finally out for the holidays, and we were going Christmas shopping—not for us, not even for friends, but for a little girl named Lauren. Lauren is a poverty-stricken five-year-old, and my family and our friends were buying Christmas presents for her that her family could not afford.

I walked into Target thinking, *What kind of toys would a five-year-old little girl like?* But as I gazed down at the list her mother had sent us through Lauren's school, I realized that it didn't have a single toy on it. Lauren had asked Santa for socks, underwear, clothes and shoes—necessities that I had always taken for granted. I can remember many occasions being disappointed by certain presents. I would eagerly grab a box labeled, "To Maddy from Santa" and rip off the shining paper to find . . . clothes. I would toss it aside. It never dawned on me that some people really don't have these luxuries. Lauren wanted as gifts the things that most kids her age would classify as a waste of wrapping paper.

My sisters and I delighted in picking out little outfits for her and choosing pajamas that had to be warm because, as my sister pointed out, "They probably don't have heat."

The real shock came, however, when we went to deliver the packages. We arrived early, at seven o'clock, to spare the little girl's mother possible embarrassment. The whole street was asleep; not even a dog barked as we approached. We drove past the dark windows of abandoned shops, tumbledown houses and trailers. Many of the houses did not have street numbers, and it was difficult to find Lauren's. Her tiny, rusty trailer sat in what seemed to be a random plot of land. They didn't have a driveway, not even a mailbox. Their ancient, dilapidated van was parked in the middle of the muddy yard among trash and broken furniture. The yard was so small that we could barely fit our car into it. The rickety wooden steps leading up to the door looked as if they would collapse under the weight of our bags, and the windows were taped over with black trash bags. Our bright red and green presents stood out against the dark, gloomy landscape.

My mother cautiously picked her way across the grassless yard and approached the steps. Slowly, she laid the bags down and knocked. She returned to the car and was about to drive away when the rusty trailer door slammed open. A woman stepped out, looking angry and confused.

"This is for Lauren," my mother explained through the car window, smiling. The lady appeared not to have heard and continued staring blankly at my mother. She hadn't noticed the bright bags at her feet. I quickly reached over and shut off the ignition. My mother got out and once again explained, "We've left something for Lauren—it's for Christmas." The lady's dark eyes softened, and she smiled. She seemed too stunned for words. Offering a simple, "Merry Christmas," we drove off, leaving the woman still standing in her doorway, smiling.

That Christmas, as I sat looking at my brightly wrapped presents, the shining tree and my happy family, I remembered Lauren. I hoped that she was having just as wonderful a Christmas with her family. I felt like we had helped to keep a little girl's belief in Santa Claus alive.

Without realizing it, little Lauren helped me learn how truly lucky I am. She taught me a lot about giving and love, and the true meaning of Christmas. That Christmas truly was a memorable holiday. Wherever Lauren is, I hope she felt the same way.

Maddy Lincoln, thirteen

Taffy Twist

The most wasted day of all is that during which we have not laughed.

Sebastian R. N. Chamfort

"How's it look?" my mother asked me. I stared into the boiling pink goo bubbling up in the pan. My mom had decided that we should have an "old-fashioned" Christmas this year, and we were experimenting with making taffy for the first time in our lives.

"I think it's ready," I said. The candy thermometer read 265 degrees. My mother checked it.

"It's definitely ready," she said. "Let's pour it out."

My little sister, Janet, had a large cookie sheet buttered and ready to go. My brother Mike and his best friend, Jimmy, looked on as my mother took the hot pan off the stove and poured the pink taffy slowly onto the cookie sheet. It looked shiny and delicious.

"While we wait for that to cool, let's pull this one," my mom said, pointing to the white taffy we'd made earlier.

"Yeah!" we shouted. It was the moment we'd been waiting for. My mom cut the white taffy into two halves and gave one hunk to Mike and Jimmy, and the other hunk to Janet and me. As teams, we began pulling on opposite sides of our taffy, making long stringy lengths, folding it in half and pulling it out again. We did this over and over until our sticky taffy turned smooth and satiny. It was hot work, but no one minded on such a cold December night in Alaska. It made us feel cozy even though huge snowflakes spun past the streetlights outside.

Now that the taffy was pulled, we rolled it into one big ball. From there, we took small pieces and formed them into little taffy "snakes." When the pink taffy was cool enough, we repeated the process.

"Now," my mother said, "watch this." She picked up a length of white taffy and a length of pink taffy and twisted them together. She pinched the ends and formed a crook at the top. "It's a candy cane!" she said.

"How cool!" we said, excited to be making our own candy canes from scratch. We got busy twisting the taffy and soon had a large batch of candy canes ready. We took them out to the living room and hung them one by one on our Christmas tree. Our tree was decorated with home-made ornaments in the spirit of an old-fashioned Christmas and the freshly made candy canes added just the right touch. We took a moment to admire our handiwork and then headed back into the kitchen to clean up our mess.

After the last pan had been washed and dried and the kitchen was tidied up, we returned to the living room to enjoy our creations and relax in front of the fire. But when we entered the living room, the sight of our tree made us stop and stare in amazement.

The homemade taffy candy canes were now two and three feet long! They oozed from branch to branch like thick pink and white spider webs.

"Oh no!" my mother shrieked. "The heat from the fire-place is melting the taffy!"

Mike stifled a laugh. That did it. In an instant, we were all hysterical with laughter as we watched the blobs of taffy slowly plop onto the carpet.

The next year at Christmas, we bought candy canes from the store.

Sandra J. Payne

THE FAMILY CIRCUS

By Bil Keane

"Santa watches for naughty stuff in December, then God takes over all the other months."

Reprinted with permission from Bil Keane.

The Drummer Boy

Give what you have. To some it may be better than you dare think.

Henry Wadsworth Longfellow

I couldn't have been more excited. The pastor and his wife were coming for dinner! I had a few favorite people in the world—and one of them was Pastor Shick. No matter where I saw him, he would always open up his big arms and give me a bear hug.

When my parents told me that he was coming for dinner, I jumped up and down with as much excitement as a seven-year-old could show. Then I realized I didn't have a present for him, and it was a week before Christmas.

Kneeling down near the wrapped gifts under the tree, I burrowed around the mountain of presents, hoping my mom or dad had left him one. Nothing was labeled Pastor Shick. Just as I was getting up, an ornament caught my eye; it was a hand-painted wooden drummer boy, about three inches tall. I thought to myself, *Pastor Shick's son, James, had played his drum during church last night while a teenager sang, "The Little Drummer Boy." The pastor must like that song to have his son play it at Christmastime.*

Hurrying, I yanked the wooden figure off the tree, grabbed some wrapping paper and ran to my mom's bedroom. Quickly, I covered the ornament with the colorful paper and began encircling the small package with Mom's entire roll of cellophane tape.

Soon the pastor and his wife arrived. We sat down at the dining-room table, and I began eating meatballs and spaghetti while the adults talked. The meal was so delicious and the conversation so interesting that I almost forgot about my gift until dessert.

Reaching under my chair, I grabbed my secret surprise. "Here," I tossed the mummy-taped gift over the table with no introduction. "Merry Christmas!"

My parents' faces went pale. They had no idea what I had given him.

The pastor reached for the gift with a smile. "How sweet of you, Michele." For several minutes he tried to unfurl the tape, then he turned to my father, saying, "I think I might need a pair of scissors. Would you have some handy?"

My father rose and grabbed a pair from a drawer.

With a few cuts and a hard pull, the minister discovered what I had bundled: the wooden drummer boy. It was very small and looked a bit worse from the tape.

"My goodness!" the minister gasped. "This is really something, young lady."

"It reminded me of last night when James played the drum," I smiled. "I love 'The Little Drummer Boy' song!"

After we finished our ice cream, the pastor gave me another warm hug, and he and his wife left. I wasn't too sure if he had really liked my gift, but I was still glad that I had remembered him in a special way.

The moment Pastor Shick was out the door, my father

turned to me and questioned, "Why did you give him that old ornament?"

"I thought he'd like it," I sputtered.

"Next time, ask before you take something off the tree," my father warned. "If you wanted to give him an ornament, you should have given him one of these big, fancy glass or crystal ones."

"Oh." Now I felt my gift wasn't good enough and my eyes fell to the floor. "Sorry."

The next Sunday, I was almost too embarrassed to go to church. I thought that my dad was probably right. I should have given him a larger ornament, one with fancy colors that glistened or twinkled with lights. After all, Pastor Shick was a very important person.

We sat in the first pew as usual, but I couldn't even look up. When it came time for the sermon, I began fidgeting in my seat, kicking my feet.

"I want to tell you all of a wonderful Christmas gift that was given to me this past week," the pastor said, holding up the familiar drummer-boy ornament. "It's one that shows that even a seven-year-old knows the true reason why we give to one another at Christmastime. Out of all of the presents I received this year, this one means the most to me. And let me tell you why. . . . For those who didn't attend the Christmas concert service, my son played his snare drum for 'The Little Drummer Boy' song. Yesterday, my son left to go back to college. Now I will keep this on my desk, reminding me that wherever he is, he is my drummer boy."

The congregation clapped.

He continued, "Over the years, I prayed to God that my family would impact your lives and that we'd make beautiful memories together. And now I know that my son's music meant something to a special little girl, as much as it meant to my family. I would like to thank her from the bottom of my heart." His eyes got teary. "She reminded me that it isn't the gift that is most important, but the love that prompted it."

After the service I went up to the pastor and received my big Sunday hug. He thanked me again for the precious ornament. Those surrounding us realized I was the girl who'd given the drummer boy gift and smiled at me knowingly.

"After I gave it to you, I was worried if you'd like it because it was so small," I finally stammered.

"Well, you're small, and I love you," the pastor said.

"But it's not fancy; it doesn't have lots of sparkles."

"Well, Jesus didn't have fancy things when he walked on Earth, but I love Him very much, too."

To this day, each Christmas when I hear "The Little Drummer Boy," I remember Pastor Shick's family fondly. That ornament was so tiny, but the meaning became larger than life to me. I learned at seven years old that it's not the gifts themselves that are important; it's making someone happy, and being willing to show love by sharing, that represent the true spirit of giving.

Michele Wallace Campanelli

Double Angels

Nothing is ever lost by courtesy. It is the cheapest of pleasures, costs nothing and conveys much. It pleases him who gives and receives and thus, like mercy, is twice blessed.

Erastus Wiman

Waking up to the sound of my alarm, I smiled at the joy of only having to wait one more day. I got out of bed and threw some clothes on. Digging around the kitchen for some breakfast, I settled on a bowl of Cheerios and some leftover pizza from the night before. After watching cartoons, playing some video games and chatting on-line with some friends, it suddenly hit me that I hadn't bought a present for my mom. It was Christmas Eve, and the stores were going to be closing pretty soon. So I threw some shoes on, grabbed my skateboard and set off to the mall.

I swung open the heavy glass door into the mall only to see an incredible sight. People were running and panicking everywhere, trying to find the perfect gift for their loved ones. It was total madness. I decided to begin trying to make my way through the crowds when a guy in a black coat came up to me and told me with desperation in his voice that he had lost his brown leather wallet. Before I could say a word, he shoved his gray business card into my hand.

"Please call me at the number on the card if you happen to find it," he said. I looked at him, shrugged my shoulders and replied, "Yeah, no problem. I'll do that."

He turned to stop another person, and I continued to make my way through the unending stream of shoppers to look for a gift for my mom. I searched everywhere, up and down the mall in every store, with no luck. Finally, toward the very end of the mall, I spotted a small antique and glass-art store. It looked like it might have some interesting stuff—not the same as I'd seen in every other store. I figured I had nothing to lose so I went in.

Papers and boxes had been thrown everywhere from all the greedy Christmas shoppers digging around for the perfect gifts. It was pretty bad. It looked like a dirty bedroom with smelly clothes scattered around in it. As I tried to make my way through the pile of stuff, I tripped over a box in the aisle and fell flat on my face. I was so frustrated and worn out from shopping that I stood up, screamed and kicked the box. It flew through the air and hit a big, high-priced clay statue, almost knocking it over. My anger had gotten the best of me, but luckily no harm was done.

As I picked up the box to put it back on the shelf, I noticed a flat, green box hidden under some wrapping paper. I opened it up to find an amazing glass plate with a Nativity scene on it. There it was, the perfect gift, just lying in some trash waiting for me to find it. It felt like one of those moments when you hear angels singing hallelujah and beams of light stream down right over the place where you're standing. I smiled broadly, gathered it up and headed for the cash register. As the cashier was ringing up my purchase, I reached into my pocket to get my money. But my pocket was empty! I began to scramble around searching every pocket when I realized I had left my wallet at home. This was my last chance to get my mom a gift since the mall would be closing in ten minutes and it was Christmas Eve. It would take me twenty minutes to skate home and back. That's when I started to panic. *Now what do I do?* I silently asked myself.

So I did the only thing I could think of at that moment: I ran outside the store and started to beg people for money. Some looked at me like I was crazy; others just ignored me. Finally, giving up, I slumped down on a cold bench feeling totally defeated. I really had no idea what to do next. With my head hanging down, I noticed that one of my shoes was untied. *Great,* I thought. *All I'd need now is to trip over my shoelace and break my neck. That'd be the perfect ending to this useless trip.*

I reached down to tie my shoe when I spotted a brown wallet lying next to the front leg of the bench. I wondered if it could be the wallet that the man in the black coat had lost. I opened it and read the name on the driver's license inside. Yep. It was his. Then my mouth dropped in awe when I discovered three hundred dollars inside.

I never even questioned what I should do. I knew that I had to do the right thing, so I found a nearby pay phone and made a collect call to the number on the gray business card. The man answered and said that he was still in the mall. He sounded really happy and relieved. He asked me if I would meet him at the shoe store, which happened to be right next to the antique and glass store. When I got there, the man was so excited that he thanked me over and over while he checked to see if his money and credit cards were still there.

I turned to drag myself out of the mall and back home when I felt the man grab my shoulder. Turning to face him,

I let him know that I hadn't taken anything. "I can see that," he replied. "I don't think I've ever met a kid like you who would return all that money when he could have taken it without anybody knowing." Then he opened up the wallet and handed me four twenty-dollar bills, thanking me again.

In great excitement, I leaped into the air and shouted, "Yes!" *I* thanked *him* this time and told him I had to hurry and go get my mom a present before the mall closed. I made it to the store just as they were getting ready to lock up. The lady was really nice about it and let me in.

I bought the glass plate and started skating home, grateful that everything had worked out. I found myself whistling Christmas carols as I replayed the evening over in my head. Suddenly, it hit me. I realized that I had been sort of a Christmas angel for the man who had lost his wallet, and that he had been the same for me when I'd forgotten mine. *Double angels!* I thought. It was another one of those moments when choirs of angels begin to sing and beams of light shine down on you. I knew that I'd never forget this Christmas Eve for as long as I lived.

The next morning, my mom opened my "miracle present." The look on her face assured me that she really loved it. Then I told her all about what happened when I was trying to get her gift. The story made the plate even more special to her.

Still, to this day, she keeps that green glass plate on our main shelf as a centerpiece. It reminds her of me, of course, but it continues to remind me that amazing things can happen when you least expect them. Especially during that magical time called Christmas.

David Scott, sixteen

The Bicycle

He did it with all his heart and prospered.

2 Chronicles 31:21

When I was nine, I needed to earn money, so I asked Mr. Miceli, the *Herald-American*'s man in my Chicago neighborhood, about an after-school paper route. He said if I had a bicycle, he'd give me a route. My dad was working four jobs then. He built neon signs in a sheet metal shop during the day, delivered flowers until eight in the evening, drove a cab till midnight, and on weekends sold insurance door-to-door. He bought me a used bike, but right after that he was hospitalized with pneumonia and couldn't teach me how to ride it.

But Mr. Miceli hadn't asked to see me ride. He merely asked to see the bike. So I walked it down to his garage, showed it to him and got the job.

At first, I slung my delivery sack filled with rolled papers over the handlebars and walked my bike down the sidewalks. But pushing a bike with a load of paper was awkward. After a few days I left the bike at home and borrowed Mom's two-wheeled steel-mesh shopping cart.

Delivering papers from a bike is tricky. You get one chance to throw each paper, and if it misses the porch or stoop, too bad. So I left Mom's cart at the sidewalk and carried each paper to its proper destination. If it was a second-floor porch, and I missed the first throw, I retrieved the paper and threw again. On Sundays, when the papers were big and heavy, I carried each one up the stairs. If it was raining, I put my papers inside the screen doors or, at apartment buildings, in the entrance halls. In rain or snow I put Dad's old raincoat over the cart to keep the papers dry.

It took me longer to make my deliveries by cart than if I were on a bike, but I didn't mind. I got to meet everyone in the neighborhood, working-class people of Italian, German or Polish descent, who were invariably kind to me. If I saw something interesting while walking my route, such as a dog with puppies or a rainbow of oil on wet asphalt, I could stop to watch for a while.

When Dad returned from the hospital, he resumed his day job, but he was too weak to work the others and had to give them up. Now we needed every dime we could raise to pay bills, so we sold my bike. Since I still didn't know how to ride it, I didn't object.

Mr. Miceli must have known I wasn't using a bike, but he said nothing about it to me. In fact, he rarely spoke to any of us boys, unless it was to give us a hard time for missing a customer or leaving a paper in a puddle.

In eight months, I built my route from thirty-six subscribers to fifty-nine, mostly because customers sent me to their neighbors, who said they wanted to take the paper. Sometimes people stopped me on the street to tell me to add them to my list. I collected every Thursday evening, and since most customers gave me a little extra money, soon I was making almost as much in tips as I got in pay from Mr. Miceli. That was good, because Dad still couldn't work much and I had to give most of my wages to Mom.

On the Thursday evening before Christmas, I rang my first customer's doorbell. Even though the lights were on, nobody answered the door so I went on to the next house. No answer. The same thing happened at the next family's house and the one after that. Soon I had knocked and rung at most of my subscribers' doors, but not one appeared to be home. I was very worried; I had to pay for my papers every Friday. And while it was almost Christmas, I'd never thought everyone would be out shopping. So I was very happy when, going up the walkway to the Gordons' house, I heard music and voices. I rang the bell.

Instantly the door was flung open, and Mr. Gordon all but dragged me inside. Jammed into his living room were almost all my fifty-nine subscribers. In the middle of the room was a brand-new Schwinn bicycle. It was candy-apple red, and it had a generator-powered headlight and a bell. A canvas bag bulging with colorful envelopes hung from the handlebars.

"This is for you," Mrs. Gordon said. "We all chipped in." The envelopes held Christmas cards, along with the weekly subscription fees. Most also included a generous tip. I was dumbstruck. I didn't know what to say. Finally, one of the women called for quiet and gently led me to the center of the room.

"You are the best paperboy we've ever had," she said. "There's never been a day when a paper was missing or late, never a day when it got wet. We've all seen you out there in the rain and snow with that little shopping cart. And so we thought you ought to have a bicycle."

All I could say was "thank you." I said it over and over.

When I got home, I counted more than one hundred dollars in tips, a windfall that made me a family hero and brought our household a wonderful holiday season. My subscribers must have called Mr. Miceli, because when I got to his garage the next day to pick up my papers, he was waiting outside.

"Bring your bike tomorrow at ten, and I'll teach you how to ride," he said. And I did.

My subscribers gave me another gift that season: a shining lesson about taking pride in even the humblest work, a Christmas present I try to use often, as I remember the kind Chicagoans who gave it to me.

Marvin J. Wolf
Originally appeared in
A 6th Bowl of Chicken Soup for the Soul

Many Times Over

The wise man does not lay up treasure. The more he gives to others, the more he has for his own.

Lao-Tse

It was a cold day in early December. I was pretty bored just sitting around the house. There was nothing on TV, my friends weren't around, and I'd read every magazine I had on skateboarding, snowboarding and every other hobby of mine. I was about to go stir-crazy when my Aunt Mary, who had stopped by to visit, asked me if I'd like to go grocery shopping with her.

Perfect opportunity to get a new magazine, I thought. There was one problem, though. I'd run out of allowance money. So I decided to ask my mom, in the nicest, sweetest voice I could, if I could have five dollars from my upcoming allowance to buy a magazine that I had been wanting really badly. To my relief, Mom agreed to the deal, and my aunt and I took off shopping.

As we were walking into the grocery store, a poor, homeless woman sat outside the doors asking customers for money donations. *Wow,* I thought. *And I was having a bad day because I was bored.* I checked on the five dollars in my pocket as I thought about the magazine that was waiting inside the store. My aunt went to do her shopping, and I headed for the magazine racks. As I flipped through the new magazines, looking for the one with the article my friend had told me about, I kept flashing on the woman sitting out in the cold without a home to keep her warm. Before I knew it, I had put the magazines back and was heading in the direction of the homeless woman. I realized that she needed the money a lot more than I needed a new magazine.

As I passed the produce section, I saw my aunt picking out vegetables, so I stopped to tell her that I'd meet her at the checkout counter. Before she could question me about where I was going, I was off and running toward the store entrance.

I stepped out into the cold air and looked to my right. Sure enough, the woman was still where she had been when we came in. I reached into my pocket, pulled out the five dollars and handed it to the woman. The look of appreciation on her face was worth more than five dollars. She was so grateful that she stood up and gave me a big hug. "Thank you, young man," she said with a shaky voice. "I can't believe that you ran all the way back here to give me your money."

"No problem," I assured her. "And, hey—Merry Christmas," I said, as I smiled and turned to go find my aunt.

When I arrived back at my house, my mom said there was some mail for me. Much to my surprise, my uncle had sent me a Christmas card—with a twenty-dollar bill inside!

I've heard it said that if you give from the heart, unselfishly and unconditionally, it will be returned to you many times over. On that cold December day, I realized how that isn't just a saying. Good deeds do come back to you.

Nick Montavon, thirteen

An Angel Among Us

Do all the good you can, by all the means you can, in all the ways you can . . . as long as ever you can.

John Wesley

I come from a large family of nine brothers and sisters, and all of us have kids of our own. On each Christmas night, our entire family gathers at my oldest sister's home, exchanging gifts, watching the nativity skit put on by the smaller children, eating, singing and enjoying a visit from Santa himself.

The Christmas of 1988, my husband Bob and I had four children. Peter was eleven, Leigh-Ann was nine, Laura was six and Matthew was two. When Santa arrived, Matthew parked himself on Santa's lap and pretty much remained dazzled by him for the rest of the evening. Anyone who had their picture taken with Santa that Christmas also had their picture taken with little Matthew.

Little did any of us know how precious those photos with Santa and Matthew would become. Five days after

Christmas, our sweet little Matthew died in an accident at home. We were devastated. We were lucky to have strong support from our families and friends to help us through. I learned that the first year after a death is the hardest, as there are so many firsts to get through without your loved one. Birthdays and special occasions become sad, instead of joyous.

When our first Christmas without Matthew approached, it was hard for me to get into the holiday spirit. Bob and I could hardly face putting up the decorations or shopping for special gifts for everyone. But we went through the motions for Peter, Leigh-Ann and Laura. Then, on December 13, something extraordinary happened to raise our spirits when we didn't think it was possible.

We were just finishing dinner when we heard a knock on the front door. When we went to answer it, no one was there. However, on the front porch was a card and gift. We opened the card and read that the gift-giver wanted to remain anonymous; he or she just wanted to help us get through a rough time by cheering us up.

In the gift bag was a cassette of favorite Christmas music, which was in a little cardboard Christmas tree. The card described it as being "a cartridge in a pine tree," a twist on the "partridge in a pear tree" verse in the song, "The Twelve Days of Christmas." We thought that it was a very clever gift, and the thoughtfulness of our "elf" touched our hearts. We put the cassette in our player and, song by song, the spirit of Christmas began to warm our hearts.

That was the beginning of a series of gifts from the clever giver, one for each day until Christmas. Each gift followed the theme of "The Twelve Days of Christmas" in a creative way. The kids especially liked "seven swans a-swimming," which was a basket of swan-shaped soaps plus passes to the local swimming pool, giving the kids something to look forward to when the warm days of spring arrived. "Eight maids a-milking" included eight bottles of chocolate milk, eggnog and regular milk in glass bottles with paper faces, handmade aprons and caps. Every day was something very special. The "five golden rings" came one morning just in time for breakfast—five glazed doughnuts just waiting to be eaten.

We would get calls from our family, neighbors and friends who would want to know what we had received that day. Together, we would chuckle at the ingenuity and marvel at the thoughtfulness as we enjoyed each surprise. We were so caught up in the excitement and curiosity of what would possibly come next, that our grief didn't have much of a chance to rob us of the spirit of Christmas. What our elf did was absolutely miraculous.

Each year since then, as we decorate our Christmas tree, we place on it the decorations we received that Christmas while we play the song "The Twelve Days of Christmas." We give thanks for our elf who was, we finally realized, our very own Christmas angel. We never did find out who it was, although we have our suspicions. We actually prefer to keep it that way. It remains a wondrous and magical experience—as mysterious and blessed as the very first Christmas.

Rita Hampton

The Twelve (Silly) Days of Christmas

On the first day of Christmas
My mother gave to me
A toothbrush I didn't really need.

On the second day of Christmas
My mother gave to me
Two pairs of new socks
And a toothbrush I didn't really need.

On the third day of Christmas
My mother gave to me
Three hairbrushes
(I guess my hair was messy)
Two pairs of new socks
And a toothbrush I didn't really need.

On the fourth day of Christmas
My mother gave to me
Four Canadian coins
(Which, as it turns out, are pretty useless 'cause
    I don't live in Canada)
Three hairbrushes
Two pairs of new socks
And a toothbrush I didn't really need.

On the fifth day of Christmas
My mother gave to me
Five Barbie rings
(They're really tiny, and I'm way too old for Barbie)
Four Canadian coins
Three hairbrushes
Two pairs of new socks
And a toothbrush I didn't really need.

On the sixth day of Christmas
My mother gave to me
Six comic books
Five Barbie rings
Four Canadian coins
Three hairbrushes
Two pairs of new socks
And a toothbrush I didn't really need.

On the seventh day of Christmas
My mother gave to me
Seven "days of the week" undies
(I hope no one from school ever sees these)
Six comic books
Five Barbie rings
Four Canadian coins
Two pairs of new socks
And a toothbrush I didn't really need.

On the eighth day of Christmas
My mother gave to me
Eight electronic games
(Enough to drive her crazy)
Seven "days of the week" undies
Six comic books
Five Barbie rings
Four Canadian coins

Three hairbrushes
Two pairs of new socks
And a toothbrush I didn't really need.

On the ninth day of Christmas
My mother gave to me
Nine candy kisses
(I really like this gift, I think I'll give
    her one of my Barbie rings)
Eight electronic games
Seven "days of the week" undies
Six comic books
Five Barbie rings
Four Canadian coins
Three hairbrushes
Two pairs of new socks
And a toothbrush I didn't really need.

On the tenth day of Christmas
My mother gave to me
Ten blue flyswatters
(My mom's losing it; what happened to the
    candy kisses?)
Nine candy kisses
Eight electronic games
Seven "days of the week" undies
Six comic books
Five Barbie rings
Four Canadian coins
Three hairbrushes
Two pairs of new socks
And a toothbrush I didn't really need.

On the eleventh day of Christmas
My mother gave to me
Eleven novelty ice-cube trays

(Now I know she's really lost it)
Ten blue flyswatters
Nine candy kisses
Eight electronic games
Seven "days of the week" undies
Six comic books
Five Barbie rings
Four Canadian coins
Three hairbrushes
Two pairs of new socks
And a toothbrush I didn't really need.

On the twelfth day of Christmas
My mother gave to me
Twelve Snoopy Band-Aids
(I scratched myself trying to get
    the ice out of the novelty ice trays—
    how did she know I would need these?)
Eleven novelty ice trays
Ten blue flyswatters
Nine candy kisses
Eight electronic games
Seven "days of the week" undies
Six comic books
Five Barbie rings
Four Canadian coins
Three hairbrushes
Two pairs of new socks
And a toothbrush I didn't really need.

Kristina Richardson

THE FAMILY CIRCUS By Bil Keane

"Her true love sure gave her
a bunch of weird presents."

Reprinted with permission from Bil Keane.

REAL LIFE ADVENTURES By WISE and ALDRICH

From the Heart

From home to home, and heart to heart, from one place to another . . .
The warmth and joy of Christmas brings us closer to each other.

Emily Matthews

Dear Dad,

I didn't know what to get you for Christmas. Actually, I don't know what you ever want for any holiday, even on your birthday. I mean, I could always get you a "#1 Dad" shirt or mug, but what dad doesn't have enough of that stuff sitting around collecting dust?

I have been concentrating extremely hard on thinking about what you would possibly want. I know you love NASCAR, but I have always gotten you racing stuff for Christmas. I tried to think of what you do for fun, hoping that might spark an idea, but I don't know what you do for fun. You are always working, Monday through Friday, and then coming home to find just more stuff that needs to be done around the house. I don't think you ever get a break to have time to do the fun activities that other people enjoy (except for Sunday afternoons, which are totally dedicated to watching cars go round and round a track for hours on end). If you are not outside taking care of the dog or mowing the lawn, you might be found inside painting or even preparing meals.

I don't know how you accomplish everything every day, working nine-hour days, completing the things needing to be done around the house, paying the bills and still having time for your family, church and going to almost all of the sporting events that we kids are involved in.

I was at the mall, looking for gifts with one of my friends, when it finally hit me. I knew what I wanted to give you for Christmas. All you have ever asked for on any holiday, including your birthday, is for everyone to get along. You don't want gifts that are purchased at the mall.

I returned home, went straight to my room and prepared the present I have decided on. I spent the whole night working on it.

Dad, I didn't get you a store-bought present this year. Here it is, the perfect Christmas gift from me to you . . . that truly came from my heart.

DAD

Mr. Fix-It,
Trying to repair it all.
Mr. Yard Keeper,
Raking the leaves in Fall.
Mr. Homework Helper,
Helping me prepare for tests.
Mr. Encourager,
Telling me to do my best.
Mr. Punisher,
Grounding me when I do wrong.

Mr. Worker,
Laboring all day long.
Mr. Cook,
Making his famous food.
Mr. Holiday Helper,
To Santa, the Tooth Fairy and the Easter Bunny, too!
However you want to say it,
In good times and in bad,
He is all these things wrapped up in one,
And to me . . . he is my DAD.

Love, Jessica

Jessica Lamb, fifteen

Snowball's Miracle

Where there is great love, there are always miracles.

Willa Cather

When I looked into her big brown eyes, my heart melted. She won me over instantly with her big sloppy kisses. That Christmas Eve morning, I received my most-wanted Christmas gift and a wonderful, new friend. Since the weather was freezing cold and the puppy was nothing but a little ball of white fur, the name Snowball seemed to be very fitting.

Snowball snuggled closely to me and went to sleep. Later that afternoon, I noticed that her eyes were turning red. She started coughing and sneezing. Her nose was running. I called the pet store where we adopted Snowball. The manager offered to refund our money or give us another puppy. The choice was ours.

"No way!" I shouted. "I already love her!" Instead, I called the veterinarian's office and explained the circumstances. The receptionist told us to come right over since they were leaving early that day for the holidays. After checking her over thoroughly, the doctor had a sorrowful expression on his face.

"It will be a miracle if this puppy lives through the night," he sadly whispered. "My recommendation would be to put her under. You should be able to obtain a full refund from the pet store."

"I won't let her die without a fight," I cried. "I'm taking Snowball home with me."

When the doctor realized how determined I was, he gave Snowball a shot and handed me a bottle of medication to take home.

All night long, I held and nursed Snowball. Together, we sat beside the brightly lit Christmas tree and watched it twinkle. I fed her chicken broth and water with an eyedropper. When I finally dozed off, even though her breathing was labored, Snowball rested contently in my lap.

I was surprised when I awoke to a fabulous Christmas miracle. Even though she was still very sick, Snowball was alive. She had made it through the night. We became best friends that day. As the days passed, Snowball became stronger and stronger. Before long, she was the picture of health.

I'm so glad that I expected a miracle to occur that Christmas Eve. She was the best Christmas gift I've ever received. Today, sixteen years later, Snowball is still alive and continues to demonstrate a zest for living. Even though Snowball can no longer see very well, her big brown eyes are still captivating. They continue to warm my heart each time I gaze into them.

Nancy B. Gibbs

A Timeless Gift

The greatness of a man can nearly always be measured by his willingness to be kind.

G. Young

Shopping for a Christmas gift can be the most nerve-wracking event of the year. Shopping for my wife can be a special challenge. Vacuum cleaners are too impersonal, football tickets are too impractical, and kitchen gadgets are downright impossible. I was at a loss, with Christmas fast approaching. In desperation, I asked my secretary, Sally, to help me pick out a present.

We walked side by side in a fast-paced walk, two blocks to the jewelry store. Working in the downtown business district had its advantages; being close to a lot of shopping places was one of them. However, there were disadvantages as well. On the way, our path crossed a couple of homeless men, huddled together by a vent from one of the nearby buildings.

I started to cross the street to avoid them, but traffic was too thick. Just before we approached, I switched sides with Sally to keep them from confronting her. They were surely going to beg for money, pretending to buy food, but any donation would surely end up as beer or wine.

As we got closer, I could see that one was probably in his mid-thirties and the other was a boy of school age—around thirteen or fourteen. Both were dressed shabbily, the older with a too-tight sport coat ripped at the sleeve, while the boy was without a coat at all, only a tattered shirt separating him from the blowing wind. *A quarter or two and they'll leave us alone,* I thought. "I'll handle this," I said with my best male bravado.

But Sally seemed undisturbed by the sight of the two beggars. In fact, she seemed comfortable in their presence. Before they asked, she offered.

"Is there anything I can do for you?" she directed her question to the two homeless men. I was in shock, waiting to pull Sally away from a dangerous situation, but she stood firm.

The two men looked at her with surprise until the older one spoke up. "Yes, ma'am. We do need something."

Here it comes—the hook, the gouge, I thought. *The two panhandlers are looking for a handout, an easy mark.* As I watched, I could tell the younger boy was shivering in the winter breeze, but what could I do?

"Could you tell us the time?" asked the older man. Sally glanced at her watch and replied, "Twelve-fifteen." He nodded his thanks and didn't say another word. We continued on our way to the jewelry store, and I had to ask Sally about the encounter.

"Why did you ask if you could help that man?"

"He was cold and in need, that's why," she replied in a matter-of-fact tone.

"But he's a bum. He could have tried to rob you or something."

"I take care of myself. But sometimes you have to take a chance on someone."

We arrived at the jewelry store, and Sally quickly found the perfect gift for my wife—a pair of diamond earrings. While she was there, she bought a man's watch, not an expensive one, but she was always thrifty. *Probably a gift for her husband,* I thought.

As we walked back to our building, the two vagabonds were still hovering around the sidewalk grate. Once again, I tried to come between Sally and the two, but she wouldn't let me. To my surprise, when we got next to them, she pulled the watch out of the bag and handed it to the older man.

"Here, I'm sure you know how to use it."

He was as shocked as I was. "Thank you, much obliged, ma'am," he said, trying the watch on his wrist. As we walked away, Sally had a gleam in her eyes, proud of what she had done.

"Why on Earth did you do that?"

Sally shrugged and said, "God has been so good to me, and I decided to do something good for him."

"But he didn't deserve it."

"Even the poor want something special, and besides, God's done things for me that I don't deserve—but He did them anyway."

"He's probably going to buy beer with that watch."

Sally just smiled at me and said, "Well, so what if he does? That's not my concern. I did something for good and that's all that matters. What he does with the watch is his challenge."

We arrived back at our building and went into our separate offices. I wondered about the encounter, and I thought about the two men. *Surely they were at the pawnshop, getting ready for a hot time at Sally's expense.*

The next day, I was going to lunch alone at a hamburger stand outside our building. As I walked down the street, I noticed the same two men that Sally and I had encountered. They were both still hovering around the heater vent. The older man recognized me and said, "Excuse me, sir. Could you give me the time?"

Aha! I had caught him. Sally's watch was nowhere to be found. Exactly what I thought.

"Where is the watch my secretary gave you yesterday?" I asked, hoping to stir his heart.

He hung his head down and admitted his guilt. "Sir, I'm sorry but I had to do something." It was then I noticed the new parka around the shoulders of his young companion. "Wouldn't you do something for one of your own?"

Speechless, I handed him a quarter and continued on my way. As I walked, I started thinking about the incident. He had sold the watch all right, but he bought a coat, not beer, with the money. Sally's act of kindness did have meaning. So did her words: The challenge was answered.

As I arrived at the hamburger stand, I suddenly lost my appetite. I turned around and headed back to the office. The two men were still by the grate. I tapped the older man on the shoulder and he looked up at me, obviously freezing. I took my long, gray overcoat off and draped it over his shoulders without saying a word. As I walked away, I knew that my own challenge had been met. The few steps back to my office made my teeth chatter. But, you know . . . it was one of the warmest trips I have ever made in my life.

Harrison Kelly

The Christmas Cookie Can

There is no surprise more magical than the surprise of being loved: It is God's finger on man's shoulder.

Charles Morgan

It was almost Christmas again, and I was in my father's home . . . one last time. My dad had died a few months before, and the home that we had grown up in had been sold. My sister and I were cleaning out the attic.

I picked up an old Christmas cookie can that my dad had used to store extra Christmas lightbulbs. As I stood there, holding the can, the memory of a past Christmas swirled through my mind like the snowflakes outside the attic window swirling towards the ground.

I was eleven years old, and with Christmas only a week away, I woke up one morning to a perfect day for sledding.

It had snowed all night, and my friends would be hurtling down the sledding hill at the end of our street. It wasn't what you would call a great challenge, but we all had fun, and I couldn't wait to try out the fresh layer of snow on the runs.

Before I could go anywhere, my mom reminded me that I had to shovel the walkways around the house. It seemed like forever, but after about an hour and a half I was finally finished. I went into the house to get a glass of water and my sled. Just as I got to the front door to leave, the phone rang.

"Joey will be right over," my mom said in reply to someone.

Geez, not now, I thought. *The guys are waiting for me.* I opened the front door, but there just wasn't enough time to get away.

"Joey, Mrs. Bergensen wants you to shovel her sidewalk," my mother stated.

"Mom," I groaned, "tell her I'll do it this afternoon." I started to walk out the door.

"No, you'll do it now. This afternoon you'll be too tired or too cold. I told her you would be right over, so get going."

My mother sure is free with my time, I thought to myself, as I walked around the corner to the old lady's house. I knocked on her door.

The door opened, and there was Mrs. Bergensen with this bright smile on her old face.

"Joey, thanks for coming over. I was hoping someone would come by, but no one did."

I didn't reply, just shook my head and started shoveling. I was pretty mad and wanted to take it out on Mrs. Bergensen. *Sure, you were hoping someone would come by. Why would they? You're just an old lady,* I fumed in my mind. At first, my anger helped me work pretty fast, but the snow was heavy.

Then I started thinking about Mrs. Bergensen and how her husband had died years ago. I figured she must feel lonely living all by herself. I wondered how long it had taken her to get that old. Then I started wondering if she was going to pay me anything for my work, and if she did, how much she was going to give me. *Let's see, maybe $2.50, with a fifty-cent tip thrown in. She likes me. She could have called Jerry, the kid across the street, but she called me. Yep, I'll be getting some bucks!* I started to work hard again.

It took me about another hour to finish. Finally, it was done. *Okay, time for some money!* I knocked on her door.

"Well, Joey, you did an outstanding job and so fast!" I started to grin. "Could you just shovel a path to my garbage cans?"

"Oh . . . sure," I said. My grin faded. "I'll have it done in a few minutes." Those few minutes lasted another half-hour. *This has to be worth another buck at least,* I thought. *Maybe more. Maybe I'll get five bucks altogether.* I knocked on her door again.

"I guess you want to get paid?"

"Yes, ma'am," I replied.

"Well, how much do I owe you?" she asked. Suddenly, I was tongue-tied.

"Well, here. Here's a dollar and a fifty-cent tip. How's that?"

"Oh, that's fine," I replied. I left, dragging my shovel behind me. *Yeah, right, that's fine. All that work for a buck fifty. What a lousy cheapskate.* My feet were freezing, and my cheeks and ears were stinging from the icy weather.

I went home. The thought of being out in the cold no longer appealed to me.

"Aren't you going sledding?" my mom asked as I dragged in the front door.

"No, I'm too tired." I sat down in front of the TV and spent the rest of the day watching some dumb movie.

Later in the week, Mrs. Bergensen came over and told my mom what a good job I had done for her. She asked if I would come over to shovel her sidewalks every time it snowed. She brought with her a can loaded with homemade Christmas cookies. They were all for me.

As I sat holding that can in my lap and munching the cookies, I figured that shoveling her sidewalk had been a way for me to give her a Christmas gift, one that she could really use. It couldn't be easy for her being all alone with no one to help her. It was what Christmas was really all about . . . giving what you could. Mrs. Bergensen gave me the cookies she made, and I gave her my time. *And hard work!* I started to feel better about the whole thing, including Mrs. Bergensen.

That summer, Mrs. Bergensen died, and it ended up that I never had to shovel her sidewalk again.

Now, years later, standing in my family's attic and holding that Christmas can, I could almost see Mrs. Bergensen's face and how she had been so glad to see me. I decided to keep the can to remind myself of what I had figured out so many years ago, about the true meaning of Christmas. I dumped the old lightbulbs that were in it into the trash. As I did so, the piece of paper that had been used as the layer between the cookies and the bottom of the can floated into the trash as well. It was then that I saw something taped to the inside of the can.

It was an envelope that said, "Dear Joe, thank you and have a Merry Christmas!" I opened the yellowed envelope to find a twenty-dollar bill . . . a gift to me, with love, from Mrs. Bergensen . . . the cheapskate.

Joseph J. Gurneak

The Unusual Package

Do not judge according to appearance, but judge with righteous judgment.

Jesus of Nazareth

The glow of the large colored lights illuminated the long strands of silvery tinsel and pinecone angels that decorated the huge tree in our classroom. Desks had been shoved to the back and replaced by rows of brown folding chairs. We had just finished our wonderful Christmas pageant. Now restless family members and friends wanted to head for home on this snowy Wisconsin evening, but they sat waiting. To them it was time to leave, but to each of us it was finally time to exchange the brightly wrapped presents piled under the tree.

Earlier in December, each of us students had pulled a slip of paper with a name on it out of an old coffee can. Then it was our job to buy a Christmas present for that person. All of us hoped that we would pull the name of our crush, or at least the name of our best friend.

The moment had finally come. One by one, our teacher handed Santa the presents, and he called out each name.

Some of the kids hurried up to the front and then sat down to tear off the paper right away. Others took their time to receive their gift, carefully removing the bow and then trying to take off the paper without ripping even one corner. Soon, all kinds of gifts, from board games, candy, scarves and mittens to small toys and stuffed animals had been opened.

I stood off to one side with my two best friends, Carrie and Megan. Patiently, I oohed and aahed as they each opened their gifts. Carrie's gift was from Kevin. This was no surprise. Everyone in school knew how Kevin had held his brother's head in a snowbank until he finally agreed to give up Carrie's name. Kevin had given her a two-pound box of chocolates, which she generously shared with Megan and me. I think Carrie was secretly hoping for something a little more personal like a bracelet or a ring, but I'm sure Kevin's mother had something to say about what he was allowed to give Carrie.

Megan's package contained a book of 365 crossword puzzles and word searches, "One for Every Day of the Year," the bright red print on the cover proclaimed. This was perfect for Megan, who happened to be the brains of our group. She rushed over to thank Shelby.

As Carrie flirted with Kevin and Megan pored over her book, I stuffed chocolate after chocolate in my mouth. I tried to appear calm and disinterested while, one by one, the pile of presents shrank.

Finally, the last brightly wrapped present was gone from under the tree, and I began to silently panic. I quickly put what I hoped was a brave smile on my face, which wasn't particularly easy to do, because I was thirsty after eating six chocolates and my mouth was already dry from anxiety.

Santa was about ready to get up and distribute candy bags to the kids in the crowd when our teacher handed

Santa one more gift. He called out my name, and I hustled to the front of the room, too relieved to even pretend to be disinterested. Santa handed me an old, sort of dirty-looking envelope. *That's weird,* I thought. *What an unusual package. Who would wrap something like this?* I vaguely remember mumbling "thank you" as someone in the crowd giggled. Red-faced, I hurried back to my friends.

"Who's it from?" asked Carrie.

I turned over the envelope and revealed, "To Barbie from Sarah," written in pencil. My heart dropped down to my toenails when I saw it.

Sarah was the middle child of eleven. Her family had moved here about two years ago. They lived in a house that would have been too small, no matter how few kids would have been in the family. Their yard was strewn with cars that no longer worked and parts of broken toys; a bicycle wheel there, a wagon handle here, a stuffed bear that their dog had probably chewed the legs off of. Sarah was nice enough but terribly shy. She wore strange combinations of clothes and had trouble with her schoolwork, especially reading. Sometimes our teacher asked me to help her.

My mother had instilled in me that I should always be polite and act as if I like a gift (even the time that I got a black and white shirt from my sister that made me look like an escaped convict).

"Feelings are more important than things," she always said. "There is nothing in the world worth hurting someone else's feelings over." So with my mother—and the entire roomful of people looking on—I was ready to act as if I had just been given the best present I had ever received.

"Maybe it's money," whispered Carrie.

"I think it's probably a poem," chimed in Megan.

But when I tore open the envelope and reached my

fingers in, I knew they were both wrong. I felt something hard in the corner. I pulled out a long silver chain. Dangling from the chain was a teardrop-shaped blue iridescent pendant with a scalloped silver border. It was truly beautiful.

I looked up and saw Sarah's anxious face across the room. I flashed her a big smile and mouthed, "Thank you." She smiled back, revealing pink candy cane–stained teeth.

That night, I received more than the gift Sarah gave me, which I still have. Even more valuable than that pretty necklace were the lessons that I learned that Christmas. I learned not to prejudge others, and that sometimes my turn will come last. And finally, that nice presents and kind hearts can come in unusual packages.

Barbara King

The Christmas Care Bear

*May no gift be too small to give, nor too simple
to receive, which is wrapped in thoughtfulness
and tied with love.*

L. O. Baird

I began to lose hope. The most treasured person in my
life was slowly slipping away. My blind, ninety-four-year-
old great-grandmother was sleeping soundly in the hospital bed. As I sat quietly with my family, I listened to the
constant buzzing of the machines that kept her alive. Her
face was pale and empty. No longer was she the cheerful
and jubilant person I had always known.

Thoughts flooded my head. *It seems like every day she gets
worse. She might not make it through Christmas.* I tried to think
of a present to give to her. Since she was blind, I would
have to get her a gift that she didn't have to see to appreciate, but that she could feel with her hands.

I remembered that when she lived with us she always
wanted to touch and play with my stuffed animals. Her
favorites were my unique collection of bears. I knew right
then what to get. *She's always wanted one for herself!* I would

have a teddy bear made especially for her.

"Grandma's Bear" is what I named the brown, furry animal . . . "Bear" for short. He was quite charming with his tiny black button nose and his big chocolate eyes. I looked forward to visiting her on Christmas morning and seeing the look on her face when I gave Bear to her.

The day came quicker than I thought. I clutched Bear in my arms as I walked to room 208 with my family. There was Grandma, propped up in her bed. Her eyes were wide open. I think she was sensing that we were coming. A grin grew on her face as we sat on her bed, close to her frail body hidden under the covers.

"Merry Christmas!" my dad said. Our family chatted for a while with Grandma until it was time at last to give her the gifts we had brought. My mother gave her fresh-smelling baby powder because she could never have enough of it. My father brought her favorite caramel candies, and my brother brought her a new nightgown. Now it was my turn. I placed the fuzzy bear in her gentle, skinny hands. Her face was suddenly filled with joy. The last time I had seen her that happy was many months earlier.

She cooed and hugged the stuffed animal the whole time we were there. She absolutely loved Bear, and she didn't want anyone to take Bear from her because she feared they'd lose him. Before we left, she thanked me numerous times. She said that it would never leave her side. From that day on, she gradually started to heal. Everyone said it was a miracle.

One month later, my great-grandmother moved back into the nursing home where she had lived before she was sent to the hospital. The nurse said that she slept with Bear every single night and never forgot him. One day when I visited the nursing home, the nurse informed me that my great-grandmother was one of the funniest and happiest residents in the nursing home. She also said that she's taking very good care of Bear. I replied, "No, *he's* taking good care of her."

Ever since my great-grandmother got Bear, her health improved. Bear was the perfect gift. She made it through Christmas when all of us believed she wouldn't.

Months later, when I turned eleven, my great-grandmother passed away peacefully in her sleep. The nurse said that she found her in the morning, still hugging Bear. It might not have been the bear that was the miracle that prolonged her life and helped her to live the rest of her life in joy . . . but I believe it was.

Molly Walden, thirteen

A Warm Bed for Christmas

Can I see another's woe and not be in sorrow, too? Can I see another's grief and not seek for kind relief?

William Blake

Police officers know that crime never stops and the police department never closes. For the third straight year, I'd drawn midnight-shift duty for the holidays. In a state of self-pity, I patrolled the silent streets, unaware that the true spirit of Christmas would touch me that night.

Christmas Eve turned bitterly cold and windy that year. An arctic air mass settled over North Carolina, plunging us into a state of paralysis. Icy blasts dropped temperatures well below zero.

It had been a slow night with few calls for service and scarce radio traffic. Even the car-to-car channel remained unusually quiet. Nothing moved on the streets, and the crisp, crystalline quality of the night air lent an edge of sharpness to the landscape.

The dispatcher's voice reverberated through the car,

READER/CUSTOMER CARE SURVEY

We care about your opinions! Please take a moment to fill out our online Reader Survey at **http://survey.hcibooks.com**. As a **"THANK YOU"** you will receive a **VALUABLE INSTANT COUPON** towards future book purchases as well as a **SPECIAL GIFT** available only online! Or, you may mail this card back to us and we will send you a copy of our exciting catalog with your valuable coupon inside.

(PLEASE PRINT IN ALL CAPS)

First Name _____ MI. _____ Last Name _____

Address _____ City _____

State _____ Zip _____ Email _____

1. Gender
- ❏ Female ❏ Male

2. Age
- ❏ 8 or younger
- ❏ 9-12 ❏ 13-16
- ❏ 17-20 ❏ 21-30
- ❏ 31+

3. Did you receive this book as a gift?
- ❏ Yes ❏ No

4. How did you find out about the book?
- ❏ Store Display
- ❏ Teen Magazine
- ❏ Interview/Review
- ❏ Online
- ❏ Bookstore
- ❏ Price Club (Sam's Club, Costco's, etc.)
- ❏ Retail Store (Target, Wal-Mart, etc.)
- ❏ Online
- ❏ Book Club/Mail Order

5. Where do you usually buy books?
(please choose one)
- ❏ Bookstore
- ❏ Online
- ❏ Book Club/Mail Order
- ❏ Price Club (Sam's Club, Costco's, etc.)
- ❏ Retail Store (Target, Wal-Mart, etc.)

6. What magazines do you like to read? *(please choose one)*
- ❏ Teen People
- ❏ Seventeen
- ❏ YM
- ❏ Cosmo Girl
- ❏ Rolling Stone
- ❏ Teen Ink
- ❏ Christian Magazines

7. What books do you like to read? *(please choose one)*
- ❏ Fiction
- ❏ Self-help
- ❏ Reality Stories/Memoirs
- ❏ Sports
- ❏ Series Books (Chicken Soup, Fearless, etc.)

8. What attracts you most to a book? *(please choose one)*
- ❏ Title
- ❏ Cover Design
- ❏ Author
- ❏ Content

TAPE IN MIDDLE; DO NOT STAPLE

BUSINESS REPLY MAIL
FIRST-CLASS MAIL PERMIT NO 45 DEERFIELD BEACH, FL

POSTAGE WILL BE PAID BY ADDRESSEE

Chicken Soup for the Soul® (Teens)
3201 SW 15th Street
Deerfield Beach FL 33442-9875

FOLD HERE

Books for Life

Do you have your own Chicken Soup story
that you would like to send us?
Please submit at: www.chickensoup.com

Comments

shattering the silence. "Charlie 182, suspicious person in front of the Radio Shack, 2364 Main Street. Described as a white male wearing a dark-colored shirt and blue jeans."

I headed toward the business district several blocks away. On arrival, I recognized the man as a local transient. He was crouched in the doorway of the business, trying to take advantage of what little wind protection it offered. His ragged flannel shirt, threadbare blue jeans and well-worn tennis shoes provided no protection from the elements, and he was obviously very cold.

Pulling up to the curb, I got out of the car and approached him.

"Frank," I said, "what are you doing out here on a night like this? Why aren't you at the Salvation Army or somewhere you can stay warm?"

He looked at me and smiled wistfully. "It's Christmas, ain't it? Well, there ain't no room at the inn. They're all full up, and I got no place to go. 'Sides, ain't you got nothing better to do than bother with me?"

"No, Frank, actually I don't," I said. "Tell you what. It's warm in my car. How about sitting in the back while I check with dispatch and see if they can find a place for you tonight?"

"Okay," he replied, "but I'm telling ya, everywhere's full up. You ain't gonna have no better luck than I did. But I wouldn't mind warming up while you try."

Frank painfully stood and hobbled toward my car, his arms still hugging his body. I patted him down and, finding no weapons, opened the back door of the car for him. I got in the front and slammed the door in the face of a renewed blast of arctic air. Again I silently cursed my luck at having to work another Christmas Eve, especially this cold and miserable one.

I called dispatch to ask the local shelters if anyone could take Frank for the night. Ten minutes stretched into fifteen. It could only mean they were having trouble locating a place. Then my thoughts were interrupted by dispatch.

"Charlie 182, I've contacted all the local shelters and churches that are taking people, and all advised they were full."

A knowing voice from behind me said, "See? I told ya it was a waste of time. Now let me outta here, and I'll be on my way. I'll find something."

He wasn't under arrest, so I had no legal right to detain him. I opened the back door of the patrol car to let him out and watched as he shuffled back to the sidewalk. Then a sudden movement caught my attention, followed almost immediately by the sound of shattering glass. Frank had thrown a rock through the plate glass window of the Radio Shack.

Frank shuffled toward me. "Look what I just went and done. I broke that window so I guess you have to arrest me and take me to jail."

"Yeah, you're right," I said. "Come on, let's go."

During the drive to the jail, Frank lapsed into his usual apologetic state following one of his petty crimes. "I'm sorry for breaking that window back there," he said, "but I didn't have no choice. It's warm in jail, and they feed you."

It was close to midnight. I knew the jail had already served dinner and Frank wouldn't get fed until morning.

No restaurants stayed open this late on Christmas Eve, but I knew a convenience store that did. It wasn't much of a dinner, but I bought him two hot dogs, a large bag of potato chips and a large cup of coffee.

Frank ate like a man possessed. As I sipped my cup of hot coffee, he devoured his meal. The combination of food and warmth worked their magic, and Frank's peaceful snores accompanied me for the remainder of the drive.

On arrival at the jail, I escorted Frank inside, completed

the booking process and left him. On my way out, I approached Frank and the jailer escorting him to his holding cell. Frank extended his hand and said, "Merry Christmas, Officer Smothers. Thank ya for everything ya done."

I smiled and said, "Merry Christmas, Frank. You're welcome."

Thoughts of Frank rode shotgun with me for the rest of the night. There were six hours remaining on my shift—six hours before I could go home to a hot breakfast, warm bed and loving family.

The next morning, I celebrated Christmas with my loved ones. Wrapping paper littered the floor, carols resounded throughout the house, and a warm fire blazed in the hearth. Yet, I couldn't stop thinking about Frank. He had been willing to commit a crime just so he could get warm for the night, and I had been feeling sorry for myself because I had to work. I experienced a wave of guilt over my feelings of self-pity the night before. And silently I thanked Frank for what he'd unknowingly given me—the gift of gratitude for all that I've been blessed with.

It was the best gift I received that year.

Elaine C. Smothers

Truly Cool

Maturity begins to grow when you can sense your concern for others outweighing your concern for yourself.

John MacNaughton

My heart was in my throat. As mom and I entered the store, I had only one thought in my mind, *I hope my pretty pink bike is still there.* It would be my first bike ever. But since it was about a week before Christmas and the stores were in total chaos, Mom gently reminded me that it was possible that the bike I wanted would be sold out.

I could feel the excitement in my stomach, and my hands were jittery. I was so anxious to get the bike. I crossed my fingers as we came around the corner to the bike section. My stomach did somersaults when I finally spotted it near the end of a long row. There it was, my big, shiny pink bike! I thought it was too clean and pretty to touch, so I stuck my hands in my pockets to keep from smudging it.

The week went by really slowly. The only thing that we were looking forward to, besides school letting out, was a charity drive that our school was doing for a homeless children's shelter. We had made little toys for the kids who were living there. I was surprised to see how many were on the list—so many who didn't have a real home where they could spend Christmas.

Still, I didn't think as much about helping them as I was thinking about my bike. I couldn't wait for winter break to get over so that I could ride my bike to school for everyone to see. I would be the cool kid for once.

While we waited in the classroom for the bus to come and take us to the children's shelter to deliver our presents, I sat at my desk writing my mom a thank-you letter. I explained how I had never wanted anything as badly as I did that bike. Just as I finished, the bus driver came into our room to let us start getting on the bus. I ended up sitting next to a guy who was getting a skateboard for Christmas. We talked about how excited we were about our big gifts.

We chatted all the way there and were still talking as we came through the shelter doors. Suddenly, my mouth dropped, and I stopped in mid-sentence. I was in shock seeing kids wearing torn-up and worn-out ragged clothes. I felt sad as I looked around the place.

Our teacher encouraged us to find a kid who was staying in the shelter and visit with him or her. I noticed a little girl sitting in a corner by herself. When I walked up, it seemed like she didn't want to say "hi" or anything, but I felt like I should say something to her. So I started out by asking her if she was excited about Christmas coming. I told her about how I was getting a bike. Suddenly, her eyes lit up, and a huge smile came across her face. She told me that she would be the happiest kid in the world if she could ever get one.

Then she explained to me what her life had been like. To say the least, she didn't have a normal childhood. She had never known what it was like to live in a real home of her own with pets and everything. Her parents had been alcoholics and constantly had money problems. They moved around often because they either couldn't pay the rent or would be thrown out for some reason. Things got so bad with them that they finally abandoned her, and she ended up in this shelter.

She no longer had anyone to call family.

I realized that her getting a bike anytime soon was out of the question. I mean, who would buy it? Her parents were gone, and she was alone in the world, other than for the people who ran the shelter. My heart just ached for her.

We got so involved in our conversation that my teacher had to come and tap me on the shoulder to tell me that it was time to leave. I grabbed my bag and told her that I hoped she'd have a merry Christmas and get everything she wanted. Before leaving the room, I looked back and gave her a little smile.

Later that night, I lay in bed remembering what the girl had told me about what it was like to live at the shelter. I thought about her life and about mine as well. All I had ever done was want and want and think that I never get enough. Now I'd met a girl my age who had barely enough to get by and took nothing for granted. I never understood when people would tell me how lucky I was. Now I finally understood.

Over the next three days, I kept thinking about ways that I could help make this girl's life better. Then on Christmas Eve, while sitting in church listening to the preacher speak, it dawned on me. I wanted to give her my new bike (which I had not yet received)!

When I explained everything to my mom, she gave me a smile that I could never fully describe—one like I have never seen before. My mom found the paper that told what children's shelter I had gone to and, on Christmas morning, we headed for the shelter with my new bike in the trunk of my mom's car.

I walked in feeling somewhat sorry that I would not be the one getting the bike, but I also felt really good inside. When I finally found her, she was sitting in the corner where I had first met her. Her head was down, and she seemed to be sad. I walked over and said, "Merry Christmas." Then I told her that I had something for her.

Her face brightened, and she smiled as she looked up at me. She looked happier than I have ever seen a kid look before. I grabbed her hand and walked her over to the door. Parked outside was my bright pink bike with a big red bow on it. I was expecting a bigger smile than what I had seen moments before, but instead I saw a tear running down her cheek. She was so happy that she was crying. She thanked me over and over again. I knew then that what I had done was truly cool. I knew I had made her the happiest kid in the world.

What I didn't know was that giving away the only bike I'd ever had would change the way I thought about things. But over time, I found that I wasn't as greedy as I was before.

I now realized that receiving a great gift gives you a good feeling, but giving from the heart gives you a feeling that's even better.

I also realized that I had been counting on that bike to make me cool. Although I never got to show up at school riding it, my mom was proud of me and so was everybody else. In the long run, that meant more to me than the bike, or looking cool, ever could have.

Brittany Anne Reese, fifteen

MR. POTATO HEAD By JIM DAVIS & BRETT KOTH

MR. POTATO HEAD ©2001 *Hasbro, Inc. All Rights Reserved. Distributed by Universal Press Syndicate.*

Hot Christmas

Effort only fully releases its reward after a person refuses to quit.

Napoleon Hill

Enticed by the smells of turkey, green-bean casserole, cranberry sauce, fresh-baked rolls and assorted pies, my guests waited for their call to the Christmas dinner table. The newest member of our family, baby Kirtley, had been fed before everyone else. We were all impressed when she said "more" to get more mashed potatoes and "hot" when we blew on them to cool them down.

As the time neared for eating, I added a paper Christmas napkin to each place setting and even lined the roll basket with one. I then lit the candles and called the group to be seated. Kirtley's mom placed her back in her high chair and put some dry cereal on her tray for a snack. We then sat down.

After we said grace and passed the food around the table, all of us tucked our heads and began to shovel food into our mouths. Silence reigned in the dining room except for the few chewing noises.

Out of the blue, a teeny voice said, "Hot."

Kirtley's mom said to her baby, "Yes, candles are hot. Good girl. That's right. You're doing a good job of using your words."

Kirtley clapped her little hands and said, "Hot," in a louder voice.

Her mother began eating again after simply saying, "Yes, those candles are hot."

Now, Kirtley thrust her body around in the chair, pointed toward the candles and shouted a giant, loud, "HOT!"

With this, we all looked up to see the roll basket on fire! Flames licked high in the air above and around the basket. Kirtley pointed to me as I ran for the kitchen with the flaming basket, saying, "Hot," one more time. And then she sighed and went back to eating her pieces of dry cereal.

After a few minutes of panic, we managed to finish eating, safely and happily, pausing often to thank our young rescuer who, with just one word, had saved our Christmas dinner.

Dottie Smith

Love Cannot Be Measured

The best of all gifts around any Christmas tree: the presence of a happy family all wrapped up in each other.

Burton Hillis

Two! Only two weeks before Christmas and there were no presents under the tree. I guess my family couldn't afford to get any this year. I knew that all our money went to pay the bills and rent and buy food for our family. I understood how important that was. But it was Christmas!

Thinking that maybe I could do something about it, I looked all over my room in every hiding place I had to see if I had any money left. Then I went into the living room and dug under all of the sofa cushions. I searched the pockets of my pants and jackets. Expecting to find at least ten dollars after all my efforts, I only found seven. I thought to myself, *Ah man! How am I going to afford to get five presents for my family with only seven dollars?* Buying cheap ones at the Ninety-Nine-Cent Store was out of the question.

A week went by, and there was still not one single present under the tree. One day during lunch, I thought about asking my parents if they had forgotten about the upcoming holiday, but I decided not to. I know how it feels not to have enough money.

That night, I prayed that someday my family could give me a very special present and that we could all live a better life—one without struggles over money.

As the days passed, I began to get depressed. To get my mind off Christmas presents, I decided to go play with my friend, San. While we were playing and talking, San asked me if I had any presents. I felt embarrassed to say no, so I told her that I didn't know for sure. Perhaps soon presents with my name would be under the tree.

I asked San, "What about you?"

San responded excitedly, "There are over ten gifts under the tree with my name on them!"

I was surprised that she had that many. Luckily, at that moment, I had to go in for dinner, so I didn't have to suffer through any more of that conversation.

During dinner, I remembered Santa. I thought that surely he would bring lots of presents for my family and me. There were only four more days 'til Christmas, so I had to be extra good, I decided. I had to give Santa a wonderful last impression!

The next morning, I made a list of presents that I wanted. The rest of the time I kept busy by helping out and being good. As long as I believed in Santa, I knew he would show.

That night, before going to sleep, I prayed again for presents for my family and me. Pretty soon, I started to feel ashamed of my selfishness. So instead, I began to pray for love and happiness and that I would continue to have such a wonderful family.

When I woke up the next morning, it was Christmas! I was so excited that I jumped out of bed and went right to the tree.

There were no presents at all!

At first I felt really sad, but then I looked around and saw my family's faces full of love and happiness as they worked together to make a special Christmas breakfast. At that moment I realized how much we loved each other.

I began to realize that Santa *did* bring me the best present I could ever have—love. Hearing the words, "I love you," and knowing that there is always someone who is there for you, no matter what, is the greatest gift anyone can ever have.

At age eight, I realized that love cannot be measured by how many presents are under the tree. Love is strong. Love is special. Love is ageless and timeless. It doesn't matter if we are rich or poor, sick or healthy. As long as we have love, we have Christmas every day.

Quynh Thuc Tran, ten

The Cat and the Christmas Star

As white snowflakes fall quietly and thickly on a winter day, answers to prayer will settle down upon you at every step you take. . . .

O. Hallesby

Tears fell from my eyes onto the posterboard below and mixed with the ink from the felt marker I was using to write "Missing: Gray tabby cat with white paws and green eyes."

Linda, my missing cat, had shared a close relationship with me ever since I had adopted him about two years before. Despite the fact that I had given him a female name (after an exam, our vet mistakenly told us he was female and we didn't find out the truth until much later), he didn't seem to mind. And even now, when we had taken him out of his familiar South Carolina neighborhood and moved him to Virginia, he seemed to bear it well. Linda continued to faithfully greet me every day when I returned home from school. But my younger sister had recently adopted a kitten, and Linda hadn't taken this change well. The image of the hurt look he had given me after meeting the kitten was still etched vividly in my memory.

One night soon afterward, he didn't come home for his evening meal, and none of my repeated calls throughout the neighborhood brought him running. The cheerfulness of the Christmas decorations on the houses failed to excite me the way they usually did. I went to bed reluctantly, certain he would turn up first thing the next morning. But I was wrong. And after two days, I started to panic.

Frantically, I dialed the local animal shelter, but no cats fitting his description had come in. So, with my family's help, I'd made and distributed the posters and even found a local radio station willing to announce Linda's disappearance and plead for his return. Every day after school, I spent hours either on foot or bike scanning the neighborhood for him and calling his name until my voice was hoarse. Every night in bed I asked God to bring him home.

By the time Christmas Eve had arrived, Linda still had not. He had been missing for eight days. After spending the church service and our Christmas Eve dinner distracted by my sadness and anxiety, I glumly went to bed where I dutifully prayed once more that God would bring Linda home. Then exhausted, I fell into a deep sleep.

Several hours later, my clock radio blinked 11:59 P.M. I suddenly awoke. It was rare for me to wake in the middle of the night; I'd always been a sound sleeper. But as I lay in the darkness, I was fully awake and consumed with a desire to get up and look at the stars outside.

For several years, I'd had a personal Christmas Eve tradition of scanning the sky for the brightest star, which I liked to imagine was the "Christmas star." Whether it was actually the North Star that led the ancient wise men to baby Jesus in the manger, I didn't know. But I enjoyed viewing it anyway, and usually looked for it before I went to bed on Christmas Eve. As I lay there wondering why I was awake all of a sudden, I realized that I hadn't even bothered to look for it this year.

Eagerly, I leapt from my bed and peeked through the blinds on my bedroom window, but I couldn't discern any stars. Then a thought came to me with surprising strength. *Try the front door. Now.*

The thought of opening the door to the icy wind outside didn't excite me, but somehow, I felt, I *had* to find the Christmas star. So I unfastened both locks and swung the door open. Shivering in my nightgown, I scanned the sky until a silvery white dot came into view. The Christmas star! At that moment, I knew that no matter where Linda was, or if he ever returned, God still cared for me.

I stared at the star for a moment, then reached for the door to pull it shut, looking down to the front stoop as I did so. And then I saw him—Linda—thin, shivering and reeking of gasoline. He sat quietly before me. His green eyes searched mine, as if to say, "I'm sorry. Will you take me back?"

Immediately, I scooped him up. But before I closed the door, I stood with Linda in my arms to gaze once more at the Christmas star. Then I said a prayer of thanks to the God who watches over all his creation—from the most distant star to the purring cat I held closely.

Whitney Von Lake Hopler

Mason's Sacrifice

The manner of giving is worth more than the gift.

Pierre Corneille

It was Christmas morning the year that my only son, Mason, was thirteen years old. I had been raising him alone for ten years now. My husband had been diagnosed with cancer when Mason was two, and he passed away when Mason was only three. The years had been tough, but my son and I had a very special bond. We were best friends, and my son was the most thoughtful and caring person I knew.

At thirteen, Mason got a weekly allowance of five dollars for keeping his room clean and doing odd chores around the house. Each payday, Mason would jump on his bike and ride to the nearby drug store to buy some candy or the latest magazine. He just couldn't seem to save his money, and so by the time Christmas rolled around, he had nothing to spend on gifts for others. I had never gotten a gift from him that was not homemade, so this year I expected nothing different.

After Mason finished opening all his gifts, he thanked me, kissed me and then slid off into his room. I wondered why he didn't seem to want to spend any time playing with the new stuff he had gotten. Caught in my thoughts, I was startled by Mason, who was now standing in front of me holding a nicely wrapped gift. I assumed that it was a project he had made at school, and I was looking forward to seeing what he had created this time. I cherished all of his gifts, just as I cherished him.

Inside the box was a brand-new pair of expensive black leather gloves, price tag still attached. The shock on my face was very apparent. As tears welled in my eyes, I asked him where he had gotten them. "At the store, Mom, where else?" he simply said.

I looked confused, as I knew that he didn't have that much money. I asked if someone had helped him purchase them, and he shook his head, held it high and said he had bought them all by himself.

After figuring out just the right questions to ask, I got him to reveal to me how he was able to buy the beautiful gloves. He had sold his brand-new bike to a friend at school, the one he had just gotten for his birthday two months earlier.

I cried just thinking about his sacrifice. Through my tears I told him that this was the most thoughtful thing he's ever done for me, but that I wanted to get his bike back for him.

He simply said, "No, Mom, please don't. Because Dad isn't here anymore, you never get a nice gift at Christmas, and you never buy yourself nice things. I wanted to get this for you. My old bike is still perfectly fine, really. Please, Mom, keep the gloves and know I love you every time you wear them."

We hung out for hours that morning, and I never removed the gloves. From that day on, I put them on so often that, eventually, I wore holes in them. But I still have them, tucked in a drawer in my closet. Once in a while, I come across them and am reminded of Mason's sacrifice. I immediately become filled with the gift of love that they represented that Christmas morning—the kind of gift that can never wear out.

Veneta Leonard

Afterword

Reading is great, and sharing time to read with others is even better. If you took time to share the stories in this book with family members or friends, we applaud you. If you didn't, we encourage you to do so during the next holiday season.

Sharing true stories can help you open up topics for discussion in a neutral, nonthreatening way. Conversation as a result of reading together can strengthen communication with others, build closer relationships, and enhance reading and literacy skills among those we love.

There are many wonderful organizations that support the habit of reading together with family members, and there are also some very helpful guides to great reading materials as well. Please utilize the following resources as you go forward into the coming year, committed to reading with others and sharing your love of good stories.

We also encourage you, if you haven't already done so, to read the stories in the *Chicken Soup for the Soul* series with your family. We especially recommend the 101 true stories in both *Chicken Soup for the Kid's Soul* and *Chicken Soup for the Preteen Soul*, which have been read and loved by millions of readers aged 9–13.

Please check out the following resources:

The National Center for Family Literacy
www.famlit.org
The American Library Association
www.ala.org
The Read-Aloud Handbook by Jim Trealese

More Chicken Soup?

Many of the stories and poems you read in this book were submitted by readers like you who read other *Chicken Soup for the Soul* books. We publish several *Chicken Soup for the Soul* books every year and invite you to contribute a story to one of our future volumes. Your true uplifting or inspiring stories may be up to twelve hundred words.

You may also submit something you have read, a cartoon or a favorite quotation. We will be sure that both you and the author are credited for your submission.

To obtain a copy of our submission guidelines and a listing of upcoming *Chicken Soup* books, please write, fax or check out our Web site.

Chicken Soup for the Soul
P.O. Box 30880 • Santa Barbara, CA 93130
fax: 805-563-2945
To e-mail or visit our Web site:
www.chickensoup.com

Supporting Kids and Families

In the spirit of making Christmas a special time for all children, especially for those in need, we will donate a percentage of the proceeds from the sales of *Chicken Soup for the Soul Christmas Treasury for Kids* to the Salvation Army Angel Tree Project. By providing Christmas gifts to kids who might otherwise not receive any at all, this wonderful service of the Salvation Army also provides an opportunity for people to help others in need. We are grateful to all those who support and participate in this project to make a difference in the lives of so many kids.

Salvation Army Angel Tree Project
c/o The Salvation Army
615 Slaters Lane
Alexandria, VA 22313
phone: 800-SAL-ARMY (800-725-2769)
Web site: *www.salvationarmyusa.org*

We also support the National Center for Family Literacy in encouraging families to spend time reading together. Their work impacts lives in countless positive ways.

National Center for Family Literacy
325 West Main Street, Suite 300
Louisville, KY 40202-4251
phone: 502-584-1133
Web site: *www.famlit.org*

Who Is Jack Canfield?

Jack Canfield is one of America's leading experts in the development of human potential and personal effectiveness. He is both a dynamic, entertaining keynote speaker and a highly sought-after trainer. Jack has a wonderful ability to inform and inspire audiences toward increased levels of self-esteem and peak performance.

He is the author and narrator of several bestselling audio- and videocassette programs, including *Self-Esteem and Peak Performance, How to Build High Self-Esteem, Self-Esteem in the Classroom* and *Chicken Soup for the Soul—Live.* He is regularly seen on television shows such as *Good Morning America, 20/20* and *NBC Nightly News.* Jack has coauthored over fifty books, including the *Chicken Soup for the Soul* series, *Dare to Win* and *The Aladdin Factor* (with Mark Victor Hansen), *100 Ways to Build Self-Concept in the Classroom, Heart at Work* and *The Power of Focus: How to Hit Your Business, Personal and Financial Targets with Absolute Certainty.*

Jack is a regularly featured inspirational and motivational speaker for professional associations, school districts, government agencies, churches, hospitals, sales organizations and corporations. His clients have included the American Dental Association, the American Management Association, AT&T, Campbell Soup, Clairol, Domino's Pizza, GE, ITT, Hartford Insurance, Johnson & Johnson, the Million Dollar Roundtable, NCR, New England Telephone, Re/Max, Scott Paper, TRW and Virgin Records.

Jack conducts an annual weeklong life-changing workshop to build self-esteem and enhance peak performance. It attracts educators, counselors, parenting trainers, corporate trainers, professional speakers, ministers and others interested in developing their ability to live more fulfilling and productive lives and to assist others in doing the same.

For further information about Jack's books, tapes and training programs, or to schedule him for a presentation, please contact:

Self-Esteem Seminars
P.O. Box 30880
Santa Barbara, CA 93130
phone: 805-563-2935 • fax: 805-563-2945
Web site: *www.jackcanfield.com*

Who Is Mark Victor Hansen?

Mark Victor Hansen is a professional speaker who has made over four thousand presentations to more than two million people in thirty-two countries in the last twenty-eight years. His presentations cover sales excellence and strategies; personal empowerment and development; and how to triple your income and double your time off. Mark has spent a lifetime dedicated to his mission of making a profound and positive difference in people's lives. Throughout his career, he has inspired hundreds of thousands of people to create a more powerful and purposeful future for themselves, while stimulating the sale of billions of dollars worth of goods and services. Mark is a prolific writer and has authored *Future Diary, How to Achieve Total Prosperity* and *The Miracle of Tithing.* He is coauthor of the *Chicken Soup for the Soul* series, *Dare to Win* and *The Aladdin Factor* (with Jack Canfield), *Out of the Blue: Delight Comes into Our Lives* (with Barbara Nichols), *The Master Motivator* (with Joe Batten) and *The One-Minute Millionaire* with Bob Allen, to be released October 2002. Mark has also produced a complete library of personal-empowerment audio- and videocassette programs that have enabled his listeners to recognize and use their innate abilities in their business and personal lives. His message has made him a popular television and radio personality, with appearances on ABC, NBC, CBS, HBO, PBS and CNN. He has also appeared on the cover of numerous magazines, including *Success, Entrepreneur* and *Changes.* Mark is a big man with a heart and spirit to match—an inspiration to all who seek to better themselves.

For further information about Mark or to inquire about a presentation, speak to Michelle Adams at:

MVH & Associates
P.O. Box 7665
Newport Beach, CA 92658
phone: 949-759-9304 or 800-433-2314
fax: 949-722-6912
Web site: *www.markvictorhansen.com*

Who Is Patty Hansen?

Patty Hansen, with her best friend Irene Dunlap, authored *Chicken Soup for the Kid's Soul* and *Chicken Soup for the Preteen Soul*. Both are books that kids, ages nine through thirteen, love to read and are able to use as guides for everyday life. Combined sales for both books are over four million copies. Patty is also the contributor to some of the most loved stories in the *Chicken Soup for the Soul* series, as well as coauthor of *Condensed Chicken Soup for the Soul* from Health Communications, Inc., and *Out of the Blue: Delight Comes into Our Lives*, from HarperCollins.

Because of her love for preteens, Patty created a Web site, *www.Preteenplanet.com*, to give preteens a fun and safe cyberspace experience where they can also become empowered to make their world a better place.

Prior to her career as an author, Patty worked for United Airlines as a flight attendant for thirteen years. During that time, she received two commendations for bravery. She received the first one when, as the only flight attendant on board, she prepared forty-four passengers for a successful planned emergency landing. The second was for single-handedly extinguishing a fire on board a mid-Pacific flight, thus averting an emergency situation and saving hundreds of lives.

After "hanging up her wings," Patty married Mark Victor Hansen and became the Chief Financial Officer for M. V. Hansen and Associates, Inc., in Newport Beach, California. She has remained her husband's business partner during their twenty-three years of marriage. Currently, as President of Legal and Licensing for Chicken Soup for the Soul Enterprises, Inc., she has helped to create an entire line of *Chicken Soup for the Soul* products.

In 1998, Mom's House, Inc., a nonprofit organization that provides free childcare for school-age mothers, nominated Patty as Celebrity Mother of the Year. In the spring of 2000, the first annual "Patty Hansen Scholarship" was awarded by Mom's House, funded by a $10,000 grant.

Patty shares her home life with her husband, Mark, their two daughters, Elisabeth, seventeen, and Melanie, fifteen, her mother, Shirley, housekeeper and friend, Eva, three rabbits, one peahen, four horses, five dogs, five cats, four birds, one hamster, thirty-four fish, twenty-seven chickens (yes, they all have names), a haven for hummingbirds and a butterfly farm.

If you would like to contact Patty:

Patty Hansen
P.O. Box 10879
Costa Mesa, CA 92627
phone: 949-645-5240
fax: 949-645-3203
e-mail: *patty@preteenplanet.com*

Who Is Irene Dunlap?

Irene Dunlap, coauthor of *Chicken Soup for the Kid's Soul* and *Chicken Soup for the Preteen Soul*, began her writing career in elementary school when she discovered her love for creating poetry, a passion she believes to have inherited from her paternal grandmother. She expressed her love for words through writing fictional short stories, penning lyrics, as a participant in speech competitions and eventually as a vocalist.

During her college years, Irene traveled around the world as a student of the Semester at Sea program aboard a ship that served as a classroom, as well as home base, for over five hundred college students. After earning a bachelor of arts degree in communications, she became the media director of Irvine Meadows Amphitheatre in Irvine, California. She went on to co-own an advertising and public-relations agency that specialized in entertainment and health-care clients.

While working on *Chicken Soup* books, which she sees as a difference-making blessing, Irene continues to support her two teens with their interests in music, theater and sports activities. She also carries on a successful singing career, performing various styles ranging from jazz to contemporary Christian in clubs, at church and at special events.

Irene lives in Newport Beach, California, with her husband, Kent, daughter, Marleigh, son, Weston, and Australian shepherd, Gracie. In her spare time, Irene enjoys horseback riding, painting, gardening and cooking. If you are wondering how she does it all, she will refer you to her favorite bible passage for her answer—Ephesians 3:20.

If you would like to contact Irene, write to her at:

Irene Dunlap
P.O. Box 10879
Costa Mesa, CA 92627
phone: 949-645-5240
fax: 949-645-3203
e-mail: *cs4kids@aol.com*
Web sites: *www.LifeWriters.com*
www.preteenplanet.com

Contributors

Most of the stories in this book were submitted by kids and adults who had read our previous *Chicken Soup for the Soul* books and who responded to our request for stories. We have included information about these authors and contributors below.

Michele Wallace Campanelli is a national bestselling author. Her novels include *Keeper of the Shroud, Margarita* and several others published by Americana Books. Her short stories have been published in over seventeen anthologies nationwide. Her personal editor/assistant is Fontaine Wallace, Instructor of Humanities at Florida Institute of Technology. To contact Michele, go to her official Web site: *www.michelecampanelli.com*.

Karen L. Garrison is an award-winning author, whose stories appear in *Woman's World, Chicken Soup for the Soul* and *God Allows U-Turns*. A wife and mother of two young children, Abigail and Simeon, Karen describes her family life as "heaven on Earth." You can e-mail Karen at *InnHeaven@aol.com*.

Nancy B. Gibbs is a pastor's wife, the mother of three grown children, Chad, Brad and Becky, and the grandmother of a precious little girl, Hannah. She and her husband, Roy, live in Georgia with three dogs, Snowball, Benjamin Franklin and Daisey, and one yellow cat, Sunshine. Nancy may be reached at P.O. Box 53, Cordele, GA 31010 or by e-mail at *Daiseydood@aol.com*.

Joseph J. Gurneak has lived in New Jersey his entire life and is currently the police commissioner for his community. During his fifty-seven years, he has met many interesting and wonderful people who have enriched his life. Through his writing, he loves sharing those "slices of life" for others to experience and enjoy. You can reach Joseph at 110 Kennedy Mill Rd., Stewartsville, NJ 08886; 908-479-6020; or via e-mail at *Jgurneak@spragueEnergy.com*.

Rita Hampton is an assistant manager at the Bank of Montreal in British Columbia, Canada. She has been married for twenty-eight years and is the mother of four and grandmother to her newest angel, Michaela. She enjoys dancing, singing, cake decorating, photography, and reading and writing. She'd like to dedicate this story to all the angels who have helped her and her family through a difficult time. Contact Rita at 27057—28th Ave., Aldergrove, B.C., Canada V4W 3A3.

Whitney Von Lake Hopler is the author of the new book, *A Creative Life: God's Design for You* (Xulon Press, 2002) and serves as an editor for *Crosswalk.com*, the largest Christian site on the Internet. She lives in Virginia with her husband, Russ, daughter, Honor, and cat, Milkshake. She can be reached via e-mail at *WhitneyVLH@aol.com*.

Harrison Kelly is a freelance Christian writer living in Bartlett, Tennessee. He has two children, Brad, thirteen, and Kristina, nine. He and his wife, Lucretia, have been married for twenty years. Some of Harrison's works have been published in the *A Second Chicken Soup for the Woman's Soul* and *Chicken Soup for the Golfer's Soul*. He has compiled a collection of his true-life stories in a series, *Stories from a Loving Father*. You may contact him at *HK@harrisonkelly.com*.

Crystal Ward Kent is a lifelong animal lover who currently resides with two former shelter cats in Eliot, Maine. She is a writer by profession and has written for newspapers, magazines and books, including *Yankee Magazine* and Guidepost Books' *Listening to the Animals* series. She owns Kent Communications, which provides writing, design and marketing services, and currently is working on a book. Contact Crystal at 46 State Rd., Eliot, ME 03903; 207-439-1235.

Barbara King and her husband of thirty-five years have three children and two grandchildren. She teaches fifth grade on the Menominee Indian Reservation. She has had two short stories published in national magazines and relaxes by making "pique-assiette" mosaics. You can e-mail her at *mhoc@frontiernet.net*.

Jessica Lamb is a freshman at Memorial High School. She enjoys volleyball, soccer, swimming and spending time with friends. Her favorite activity is being on the dance team at school. She has had a few of her poems published in the past. This is her first story to be published, and she dedicates it to her dad because he is always there for her.

Veneta Leonard resides in Crown Point, a quaint, historic town in northwest Indiana where she enjoys reading spiritual and inspirational writings. With an associate degree in business management, she hopes to return to school someday. Right now, she enjoys the most important job she will ever have—being a mom!

Maddy Lincoln is thirteen years old and the second of four girls. She loves gymnastics, skiing, singing and writing. She hopes to become a famous author some day. Maddy would like to thank her English teacher, Mrs. Adler, and her family for all their help and support.

Megan McKeown is a seventh-grader who lives in Olean, New York, with her mom, dad and three sisters, Molly, Kelly and Kaitlyn. She likes to play soccer and basketball. She also takes tap and jazz lessons and helps teach a class of younger children. Her favorite subject in school is language because she loves to express herself through writing.

Nick Montavon, age thirteen, likes learning to skateboard and hanging out with his friends. Nick enjoyed being in Mrs. Beth Bennett's reading class this year because of her ability to teach great lessons and her dedication to her work. He thanks his parents for always keeping him on track in his early life.

Sandra J. Payne has written several episodes of the television show, *Barney & Friends,* as well as the video, *Be My Valentine, Love, Barney,* and a book called, *Barney, I Did It Myself.* When she's not writing, Sandra travels as much as possible. She's happy to live with her husband, Perry, in Southern California as winters in Alaska are mighty chilly! Sandra can be reached at 11271 Ventura Blvd., Suite 317, Studio City, CA 91604 or e-mail her at *SJPwriter@aol.com.*

Denise Peebles is married and a mother of two children, Ashley, seventeen, and Jonathan, seven. She has been published in different e-zines and in her local newspaper. She has a story featured in the *Lauderdale County Book of History.* Her favorite topic to write about is her life and her family. It has been her dream to be a nationally published author, and now she is! You can contact her at *Speeb47489@aol.com.*

Brittany Anne Reese is a sophomore in high school whose favorite class is English. She enjoys dancing and hopes to get a dance scholarship and pursue a career in dancing. She'd like to thank her family for their support and putting up with her prancing around the house for hours at a time.

Kristina Richardson is a wife, mother of two and an adventurer. She is also an amateur writer and a photographer. You can e-mail her at *Krissi6363@aol.com.*

David Scott is a sixteen-year-old whose hobbies include skating, fishing, skim boarding and surfing. He learned how to write and gained writing experience in his writing classes at school.

Dottie Smith is a real turkey. She was born on a snowy Thanksgiving Day. When she grew up she became a nurse, but also longed to do something creative. So she began to write for children. Her stories and articles have been published in numerous children's magazines. She lives in a noisy house with an African gray parrot, a cat named PK, a dog named Taylor and her husband, Bob. She has two grown children and four grandchildren. She can be reached at 708 Calvert Ave., Clinton SC 29325 or via e-mail at *dmdsmith@hotmail.com.*

Elaine C. Smothers is a former police officer turned freelance writer. She dedicates this story to her late mother, Joyce Carter, a woman of strong character and indomitable spirit. She lives in eastern North Carolina with her police-officer husband, stepson and their menagerie of animals, and enjoys sea kayaking, camping and reading. She can be reached via e-mail at *SeaDream91@aol.com.*

Storm Stafford is a student at the University of Hawaii Manoa. She plans to teach Women's Studies when she graduates.

Quynh Thuc Tran is a ten-year-old who lives in a small city in California where she attends elementary school. She likes to draw and read during her free time and loves to write mysterious stories. Living in California has inspired her to write stories and poems about all there is to do.

Molly Walden is an eighth-grade honor-roll student in Orlando, Florida. She enjoys writing poetry and stories, acting, rowing (crew) and swimming. Her academic goal is to get her master's degree in biology/animal technology. Molly's story, *The Christmas Care Bear,* was inspired by her ninety-four-year-old great-grandmother, whose lessons of love, support and compassion have been instilled in yet another generation.

Marvin J. Wolf has written as a professional since 1965, and his byline has appeared in periodicals and bookstores in at least 132 nations. He is the author, coauthor or ghostwriter of a dozen books and hundreds of magazine and newspaper articles, as well as of marketing, advertising and business literature. The American Society of Journalists and Authors (ASJA) honored Wolf with their prestigious Robert C. Anderson lifetime achievement award in 1994. He was ASJA runner-up Author of the Year in 1995. He has also been honored by the Greater Los Angeles Area Press Club, the U.S. Marine Corps Combat Correspondents Association, the Orange County [California] Advertising Federation, the IABC, the Southern California Business Communicators and the Pacific Industrial Communicators Association. He can be e-mailed at *Marvwolf@attbi.com.*